*The person who really wants to do something,
finds a way*
(Author unknown)

Review Request

If you would recommend this book to others,
please consider writing a 5 star review on <u>Amazon.com</u>.

Make Money Online Using Zazzle

Make Money Online Using Zazzle

Internet Marketing Tips to Earn a Passive Income

TRACY FOOTE

TracyTrends

New York, USA

KidsandMoneyToday.com

Visit our website for our links to social networks:

Printed in the United States of America
Copyright © 2014 by Tracy Foote
Published by TracyTrends
http://TracyTrends.com
Please send all inquiries to:
TracyTrends
c/o T. Foote
27 West 86 Street, Suite 17B
New York, NY 10024
tracytrends@aol.com

Business & Economics / E-Commerce / Internet Marketing
Business & Money / Small Business & Entrepreneurship
Print Version ISBN 10: 0-9814737-6-8
Print Version ISBN 13: 978-0-9814737-6-5
Library of Congress Control Number: 2014905190
Connect on social networks or comment on our blog at:
http://KidsandMoneyToday.com

Contents

Become a Member of
Make Money Online Using Zazzle

You'll Receive:

- Access to our hand picked Zazzle tutorial videos
- Online marketing strategies
- Access to links and other references that you might want to copy/paste from pages in this book
- Access to more marketing links

View the link below to join:
http://KidsandMoneyToday.com/zazzle-member/

Just one of many products you might create on Zazzle:

Preface

When people ask me if I'm making money with Zazzle, my answer is always, "Yes." But what they really want to know is, "Can they make money with Zazzle and how much?"

Zazzle is one of many Print on Demand (POD) websites with the potential to boost your family income. There are two main paths to earn an income using Zazzle. You can choose to do only one, or you can choose to do both:

- *Designers:* Photographers, illustrators, artists, and writers can create products with original designs and sell them. There's no need to open a merchant account, set up any "Buy Now" buttons, or produce and ship items.

- *Affiliate Marketers:* Commissions can be earned through referrals. You send customers to Zazzle using a tracking code, and you earn a referral commission on purchases they make.

U.S. taxpayers have an additional way to boost their income because they can take advantage of small business tax laws. If you're an international reader, you might skim this section to see if any of your own country's laws might be similar.

Someone once described Zazzle as having an excellent business model. The company simply gets other people to design products, and has these same people or another group of people drive the traffic. This sounds a little sarcastic. It implies that Zazzle isn't doing any of the work, and instead, is riding on the coattails of designers and affiliate marketers. There is some truth in this.

However, it's not like Zazzle isn't paying the creators and marketers. That's how we earn our income. We take advantage of the business opportunities offered by Zazzle.

And of course, Zazzle is contributing. Zazzle researches and negotiates for new products. The staff deals with customer issues such as processing credit card transactions, overseeing shipments, and handling complaints or returns. Technicians maintain the site, ensure the pages load quickly, and so on. You might think of Zazzle as a partnership or a teamwork approach to business. We do our part. Zazzle does theirs and we both make money.

When you think about earning money with Zazzle, try to identify your goal. How much money do you want to make? Enough for a movie every weekend? For monthly extracurricular activities? A gym membership? For your mortgage or rent? An annual salary? To leave money for your heirs?

You can do all of these, but you will have to work for it. It's not free money. Store owners work both part and full time, and they report incomes reflective of the hours they put in. Zazzle has a Pro-Seller Program of six levels. It's calculated from total life-time sales on the Zazzle.com website. You reach the lowest level at $100 in sales, and you can reach *Diamond* level when your total lifetime sales are over $500,000. Zazzle wouldn't need six levels, if people weren't making money.

Your level of income will also depend on the experience you bring to the table and the amount of time you are willing to dedicate. You might find that your fastest way to make money with Zazzle is to start as an affiliate and create products later. Perhaps you have a strong marketing background, or maybe you have a large number of followers on a social network that you could tap into for sales.

If you have no marketing experience, that's acceptable too. Use your current skills of drawing, painting, graphic designing, photography, or writing to create products and launch your business. As your business grows, you will learn about marketing.

Some sellers choose to only create products. This can work if your items are unique, high quality, and have little competition. However, if you focus on even just a little marketing, it should be like giving yourself a pay raise.

Is Zazzle passive income? Yes and no. In the strict sense, it will not be passive because you should be continually marketing or creating new products. This establishes a *growing* business. However, each time you create a quality product, that particular product should continue to earn income while you sleep—and that's passive income.

This book does not make any promises of actual income. This book will help you get a faster start on Zazzle by outlining a business model that increases your potential to make sales.

~Hope to see you on the Zazzle forums,

Tracy Foote,
http://zazzle.com/tracytrends*/

Why Zazzle?

Zazzle is one of the many Print on Demand (POD) websites found on the Internet. You can establish your Zazzle account for free and start to create or market products in under an hour.

However, you might take some extra time to put some thought into your business plan rather than jumping right in.

There are numerous reasons people choose to establish their business on Zazzle. Here are some of them:

1. *Free Start-up:* Essentially, you can start your own business for free when you choose Zazzle.

2. *International Marketplaces:* Zazzle has a customer reach similar to Amazon.com. There is a Zazzle.ca, .de, .uk, and so forth, for international locations. When you create a product, the product automatically appears on the international sites (except if an item is U.S. exclusive). This means more exposure for you, more potential income.

3. *Choose your own royalty:* You set your price at Zazzle. This means you decide if you want a royalty mark-up of 5%, 30%, 99%, or something in between. This gives you some control over your earnings.

4. *You can be an Affiliate Marketer:* Zazzle refers to you as an *Associate.* You earn 15% for referral commissions. You can earn these commissions on your own products too.

5. *No Minimums:* When you open your Zazzle account, there is no requirement to sell a certain amount in a certain number of days, to create a minimum number of items, or to bring a certain number of visitors to shop on Zazzle. You can run your business as you see fit, on your own schedule.

6. *Part or Full-time Passive Income*: Items that are created and promoted well have the potential to keep earning income with little or no additional marketing.

7. *30 Day Return Policy:* Zazzle's flexible return policy encourages customers to buy products, because they know they have a satisfaction guarantee.

8. *Opportunities for Quality Products:* While many designs already exist on Zazzle, there are also many poor quality designs. You only need to create better products than the competition to rank well and increase your potential to make a sale.

9. *A Free Promotion Team:* When you create quality products, associates will choose to promote you. This is like having a free marketing department, a staff of people working for you for free.

Nothing is ever perfect. Here are some challenges to be aware of when with working with Zazzle:

1. *Location:* You are building something on a location that you don't own. It's like building your house where someone else owns the land. The owner has the ultimate decision-making control. If the owner says your curtains must be white or move your house, you'd better make your curtains white.

2. *Branding Your Business:* In general, Zazzle no longer offers the ability to customize your store. You cannot use your own background colors to match a website you already own or add very much personalization. But, you can add your own banner and category thumbnail images.

3. *Pricing Limitations*: You have no control of the base price of items. You can set your own royalty markup, but you must be aware that any base price change can boost your items into an "expensive" range, which in turn might impact your potential to earn income.

4. *Bonus Rules*: You have no control of the Volume Sales Bonus (VSB) rules. These changed in 2013, so we wouldn't expect a major change for a while, but it could happen.

5. *Potential Copyright Infringement:* By placing your designs online, there will most likely be some unauthorized "borrowing" of your images. Stolen images become a factor of doing business.

6. *Perceived Inequities:* There will be times where something appears unfair to you, and you will have to ignore it and move forward.

   Example: If a designer sets a 10% royalty, an associate promoting the same product will earn a 15% referral commission when the item sells. This is more than the designer. Some designers perceive this as unfair.

   However, the designer is responsible for choosing the low royalty rate. In addition, some would argue that designers only have to create their item once, whereas an associate must continue to promote on a daily basis to make sales.

7. *You're Alone (Sort of):* If you were used to the workplace atmosphere of colleagues, and now you decide to work Zazzle full-time from home, you might miss having some random chit-chat. One solution is to visit Zazzle's forums and make some new online acquaintances.

8. *No Income Guarantee:* You can't be sure you will have the same amount of sales from month to month, so it becomes very important to have some sort of savings. Perhaps before you quit your current job, you should save up an emergency fund equal to 6 to 12 months of income.

You might obtain a Zazzle income faster by starting with the Associate program. Because you eliminate the time required to create items, you often have a better Return on Investment (ROI), the amount of cash received for the amount of time you put in. Plus, it's nice to have income coming in while you're creating products.

Even if you're an artist and intend to only use Zazzle as a place to generate hobby income, we suggest you do not jump around the book. We think it will be most beneficial to read the material in the order presented, regardless of which income path you ultimately decide to pursue.

Getting Your Business Started

The Zero Balance Business Plan

It's easy to get caught up in the excitement of starting a business. It's common to think, "I'm a business. I need business cards, a new computer, scanner, software, and more,"and soon you are spending more than you are earning.

We suggest practicing a "Zero Balance Business Plan." This means unless you have profits to cover an expense, you do not make the purchase. The only exception should be an expense that is absolutely required for the business to run or is purchased to protect your business.

If you have no sales, wait to purchase business cards. They are wonderful to have, but not an essential start-up purchase.

You will need a computer, but you could use one at your public library. You don't have to buy one. You will need a Zazzle account which is free, and you'll also need a method for Zazzle to pay you.

You may also need a business license, but this can also wait. Technically, you do not have to declare yourself a business until you have an income. There's nothing financial to report.

Banking and Payments

Your payment from Zazzle will come by check or through PayPal. We recommend PayPal.com, so if you do not yet have an account, go ahead and set one up. It's free.

Zazzle sends you a payment when you meet your payment threshold ($50 for a PayPal payment). Payments are a sum of all cleared royalties, referrals, and Volume Sales Bonus. There is a 30 day "clearance" period which allows time for customers to return their purchases (based on Zazzle's 100% satisfaction guarantee). This also ensures that you are never over-paid. Payments are issued around the 15th of the month. Add these two factors together and in general, you have a 45 day waiting period before you receive payment for a sold item.

As you build a *cleared* Zazzle balance, you will have the option to use this "credit balance" to pay for items you might purchase through Zazzle. These items could be for either personal or business use. You can find more details under: "How to use your earnings as store credit" at Zazzle help:

http://zazzle.custhelp.com/

This may seem like a good idea, because instead of using your own cash, you can use your pending paycheck to pay for items. It's like you're being paid early. However, this can turn into an accounting nightmare. It becomes very hard to track your earnings, because they become a mixture of payments and credits applied to purchases.

If you are the type of person that will match your end-of-year report (for U.S. citizens, tax Form 1099) issued from Zazzle to your own accounting records, you will have a much easier time if you *do not* use the Zazzle credit feature.

We also suggest you have a separate credit or debit card to use exclusively for business purposes. This makes it very easy to track your business expenses because they will all be on one card. You can apply at your local bank or look for offers from PayPal.

Consider Separate Zazzle Accounts

The second rule in starting a Zazzle business is to *treat it like a business*. Always consider the thought of one day selling your company. Hence, your business cannot be your baby. You would not sell your child. Try not to get so attached to your company that selling it would be emotionally difficult.

Everyone using Zazzle has an account. You use your account to make a purchase, open a store, or collect affiliate commissions. Each account has the capability of opening multiple stores. However, at the time of this writing, you can only change ownership of an account. Zazzle does not offer the option to separate stores from an account. For this reason, we recommend owning only *one store per account*, one store per email address used. This keeps the door open for the possibility of selling your store.

Your Targeted Audience

Many small businesses work backwards. Their thought process is: "I like *this*, so I'm going to create it, and then find someone to buy it." Instead, a better focus would be: "I know people are looking for *this*, so I'm going to create it and make lots of money."

Before you open your store, spend some time browsing the Zazzle marketplace and the Zazzle forum. This is your brainstorming time. Take a piece of paper and begin writing some notes about your business idea.

What raised your curiosity about Zazzle? How did you think you could earn an income?

Maybe you are an artist and love to paint, or you're a graphics designer or photographer looking to sell your work. Are you a writer who can create great unique sayings to use on invitations, sympathy, thank you, or other type of cards?

You might browse the Zazzle *Show Me* Forum to gain some inspirational ideas of what you might create on Zazzle using your own skills. Here are some links (URLs) to check out:

- Best-sellers:
  http://zazzle.com/bestsellers
- What sells:
  http://zazzle.com/sell/designers/whatsells
- Most wished for by product type:
  http://zazzle.com/pd/mostwishedfor
- Featured Picks
  http://zazzle.com/featured+picks

It's tempting to jump right in and start creating, but if you spend time observing the types of items that appear to be selling and identifying a target audience, this should position you better for a successful Zazzle income.

The focus should be on maximizing your Return on Investment (ROI). Maybe you love designing geometric shapes and experimenting with color. You can jump right in, spend hours creating products, and you will feel good — at first, because you've accomplished something. But, if you don't know who is going to buy your item, it can be difficult to make a sale. Your return on the time invested will be very small, and you may become frustrated and quit. We don't want this to happen to you.

Your Store Name

After you've researched your target audience, you want to think about your store name. Choose your store name carefully. Once you use a store name, it cannot be used again. It's useful to use some keywords in your store name. If you find that your first choice is not available, even though you don't see a Zazzle store using that name, this most likely means the owner has not yet created items in their store or the store is private. In such case, you will have to choose a different name.

How will you spell the name of your store? Can you add an "s" to the end of your store name? This can create confusion. If you open "My Sweet Kid" on Zazzle and someone else comes along and opens "My Sweet Kids," how will you feel?

When you find a name that is available, before opening the store, do some research on the Internet. Is your store name already used on Google+, Facebook, Pinterest, Twitter, or YouTube? If so, you probably want to come up with a different name.

Is the ".com" version of your name available? For example: Is MySweetKid.com available? If not, you should probably choose a different name. You don't wan to be confused with another brand.

Securing Your Business Name

Once you've decided your store name, open an account on Zazzle using a unique email address and open your store.

Next, assuming YourBusinessName.com is available, you want to purchase this domain name. There are many places to do this. We suggest using:

http://danjo.ca/

Ask the company that registered your domain to set it up to redirect to your store URL (change *StoreName* to your store name):

http://Zazzle.com/StoreName*/

While domain registration is technically not a mandatory expense at the start of your business, it protects your business name for the future, so we think this is the first expense you should consider. You are investing in yourself.

Your domain name will be a recurring annual fee, and thus, we want to make sure your business earns at least the cost of the domain registration. Under a Zero Balance Business Plan, this would be your first annual goal: earn enough income to pay for your domain name.

Add Your Google Analytics Code

Google Analytics is a bit of coding you add to your store to track and report visitors' actions. You can sign up for a Google Analytics account here:

http://google.com/analytics/

Set up your Google Analytics tracking code. At this point, don't worry too much about how to use and evaluate Google Analytics. Instead, just create an account, get your tracking code, enter it into your Zazzle store, and let it begin tracking data.

If you need help with Google Analytics, ask someone to assist you or you might try these helpful links:

http://zazzle.com/sell/designers/tutorials/googleanalytics
or

http://ehow.com/how_8209213_track-zazzle-analytics.html

Your tracking code will be in the format of:

UA-XXXXXXX-X

Copy this code. Go to your *Zazzle Account > Store > Settings > Edit Settings*. Check the box "Enable Google Analytics" and paste in the code. (See next image.)

You will also see a box about Cross Domain Tracking. This is used if you were to place the same Google Analytics code on more than one website. For example, if you had a blog, you could place the same tracking code on both your blog and Zazzle store. We do not do this because we prefer not to mix Zazzle and blog visits together. We use a separate tracking code for our blogs. (To set up a separate code, you would go to Google Analytics, create a new Profile, and obtain a new code to add to your blog.)

Visit your store a few times from different computers on different days. The following day, login to Google Analytics and look to see if your reports show visitors. You should see some traffic in your statistics and this lets you know that your tracking code is working properly.

Don't worry about anything else right now. Don't spend time browsing around the reports. Just let the stats begin to collect. Once you have some data collected, you can come back, evaluate, and make some changes based on your predictions.

Set up StatCounter

You might also set up StatCounter. This is another tracking system with easy to read reports. Zazzle provides detailed instructions on setting this up here:
http://zazzle.custhelp.com/app/answers/detail/a_id/852

You can have both StatCounter and Google Analytics enabled at the same time. The settings are in the same place: Go to your *Zazzle Account > Store > Settings > Edit Settings*.

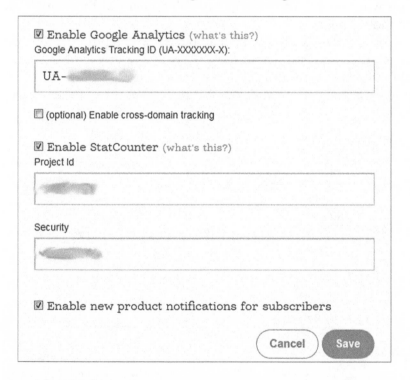

You will visit the StatCounter website to view these reports. Because they are fairly self-explanatory, we do not cover StatCounter reports in this book, so if you have questions, we suggest you post them in the Zazzle forums.

Setting Up Social Media for Traffic

After your Zazzle store is opened and you've registered your domain, consider opening social media accounts using your business name. This will begin to establishing the *social authority* of your business, which is an important step towards building your brand. People will begin to identify and differentiate your business from others. When your company name is mentioned, you want people to begin to say, "I've heard of that" or "That sounds familiar."

Not only does social media help build your branding, it can also generate traffic. Each social site will act as a doorway or additional funnel path toward a sales conversion. Here's a flow chart that might illustrate a typical Zazzle business model or a business plan.

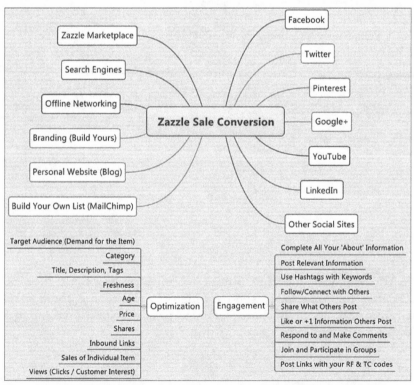

Note: Keep in mind that only Zazzle knows for sure what impacts ranking and sales. For everyone else, it is an educated prediction.

Your initial social media goal will be to establish your presence and secure your business name. You can come back later to begin engaging. It is important not to postpone setting up social sites, as it can become frustrating if you wait and find your business name is no longer available. At a minimum, you want to own:

- YourBusinessName.com
- Twitter.com/YourBusinessName/
- Facebook.com/YourBusinessName/
- Plus.Google.com/YourBusinessName/posts/
- YouTube.com/user/YourBusinessName/
- Pinterest.com/YourBusinessName/
- Linkedin.com/in/YourName/

The number one goal of social media is always a click through—to have the user click through a link and visit your Zazzle store. You are marketing on social media to make money.

Some best practices for social media engagement are:

- *Tell:* Complete every option in your Profile: all titles, descriptions, links, and any other options. Use keywords. For your description, state how you solve a problem, how you can be helpful or valuable to the person who will read your Profile. Add your store URL using this format:
  http://Zazzle.com/StoreName*/

- *Connect:* Follow other members on the network

- *Share Others' Information*: Share relevant posts that have value to your target audience and contain your keywords.

- *Share Your Referrals:* Use your referral code to share both your own and other store owners' products. Be sure to also share your store home page, categories, and departments. These last three will show in your Google Analytics reports.

- *Like other people's posts:* Click *Like, Favorite, +1,* etc.)

- *Comment:* Leave comments and respond to others

- *Be Relevant:* Post relevant and valuable information

- *Community Participation:* Join Groups or Communities

- *Don't Spam:* Aim for a ratio where the sum of all video, article, and shared posts exceeds the number of "sales" posts

We are confident that on your own, you can figure out how to open social media accounts. Instead, we're sharing some unusual tips that we've found valuable. They will make the most sense, after you've opened your social media accounts.

Hashtags

The hashtag symbol of # is used on many social media networks to connect niche discussions together. The proper way to use the hashtag is to place it before your keyword with no space, as in: #NewYorkCity. This makes it a clickable link on some social sites. When someone clicks the hashtag link, they see all the posts currently using that hashtag. You essentially tie your post to other related posts. This can give you more exposure.

You might also use #StoreName to tie all your store posts together or #YourDesignCode to tie a group of specific designs together as a collection. When the hashtag is clicked, the user would see several posts containing matching items.

It's good practice to use hashtags in all your social media posts and also in your Zazzle item descriptions. This way, if an affiliate pulls your item from Zazzle along with its description, you'll have increased your chance for extra exposure.

Twitter

Twitter differs from the other social sites because it is very *in the moment*. If your Tweet is not noticed immediately, it may never be seen. This doesn't mean you should ignore Twitter. Due to a recent change, images now appear right within your feed. Since people like to look at images, this new display format may help your products attract attention and increase clicks to your store.

Two Links on Your Profile Page: In your Twitter settings, you have an option to add a website. Enter your store URL in this format where the * is referred to as a Zazzle Star:

http://Zazzle.com/StoreName*/

The Zazzle Star makes this a *referral URL*, which we will discuss in detail later.

Your Bio is located beneath the website option. Also add your store URL there. When visitors view your profile, they will see *two clickable links*. Your Twitter Bio is also publicized by Twitter, so this link may be found outside of Twitter. It is another possible path to help get your business discovered.

At the moment these two URLs are the same, but later you can use one slot for your blog URL or a link to opt-in to a newsletter or subscriber list.

Facebook

Create a Facebook Page (as opposed to a personal Profile) and use your business name. To create your page, visit this URL:
http://Facebook.com/about/pages

Secure Your Unique URL

Keep an eye out for the screen to offer you the option to:

> *"Choose a unique Facebook web address"* to make it easier for people to find your Page. Once this is set, it *"can only be changed once."*

Enter the name of your business. If you completed the research step (described earlier), then your name should be available. If it's not available, try to use something very closely related, perhaps with an abbreviation.

A visitor is more inclined to "Like" a page that other people have "Liked," so try to increase your number of "Likes." Go to your Facebook Profile and invite all your friends to "Like" your Facebook business page.

You can also search the Zazzle forum for Facebook discussions and swap "Likes" with other store owners. While these people are probably not your buying audience, they can help add some social credibility to your page by increasing your "Likes" count.

List Your Pages on Your Facebook Profile:

Go to your Profile. Click *About* and completely fill out all entries. Next, look for the *Note* section. Click *Add Note*. Write the *Title* as a message such as "Please Like (or visit) my FB Pages." Go to the *message box* and list your pages as HTML links written in code like this (but replace *FacebookPageName* with your Facebook page and *PageName* with your company name):

<a href="http://facebook.com/FacebookPageName">PageName</a>

The result is a little block on the left of your Profile where the *Title* will be a clickable link with your pages listed, and if someone clicks this title link, then your pages also become clickable links.

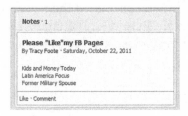

Manually Scheduling Facebook Posts (for Free):

When you create a post on Facebook, click the little clock at the bottom of a post to open the *Schedule Post option*. Choose your date and time and click *Schedule*. (We will discuss auto-posting options later.)

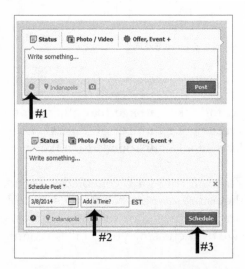

Display Facebook Comments as Posts:

To make your page more interesting and increase your potential for engagement, you might allow comments to appear as posts on your page. Go to *Edit Page > Edit Settings > Post Visibility > Edit*, and from the drop-down menu, select "Allow Posts by Other People on My Page Timeline." Click *Save*.

At this point, all comments will be visible, but the visitor must choose to see them by using the drop-down menu located below your banner, in the center of the page:

Many users don't even know they can choose to see only *highlights*, *posts by the page*, or *posts by others* (which are comments the page received). To make your comments more visible, so they appear immediately to all visitors who view your page, go to *Edit Page > Use Activity Log*. Find each comment post. Click the edit button in the upper right corner of the comment to open a drop-down menu. You will see *Default (allowed)* is checked and you want to change it to *Allowed on Page*.

If you want even more exposure, you might choose to highlight a post, which makes it fill the entire width of your Facebook page.

You'll have to manually click and edit each post to make the comment appear on your page. If you have many comments, this process is time consuming, but it might encourage more engagement on your page, and Facebook likes engagement.

Google+

Google+ is often referred to as a ghost town compared to other social sites, but this simply means there will be less competition for you to reach your target audience. You should join, even if your initial purpose is solely to secure your business URL. First, you will establish a Profile using your real name. Next, you create a Page using your business name.

Google+ allows you to group people in *Circles,* and you can post to all circles or a specific circle. This gives you the potential to target and reach niche audiences. Each circle is essentially a list containing a group of people with a common interest. When you post to a specific circle, the members receive a *notification* (assuming they haven't blocked notifications). Doesn't this sound like a free advertising opportunity?

Begin on Google+ by growing your followers. Begin with the typical strategy of looking for posts that contain your keywords, and see if these people might fall into your target audiences. Add them to your circles and engage with them.

Google+ also has the ability to *Share a Circle.* You can take advantage of this feature to quickly grow your followers and create your own niche circles. This strategy has the feel of a childhood chain letter, so it may or may not appeal to you. When you received a chain letter, you were instructed to add your name to the bottom of the list and send the letter off to five friends, who would then repeat the process. You can do something similar with shared circles.

> *Example:* Run a search for "shared circle keyword" (replace keyword with your own) to find a circle that someone else shared. They have already done all the hard work for you. Next, click the *Add People* option to quickly add the entire targeted group to your circles. Some of these people will surely follow you back.

> At this point, you'll have gained a few new followers and a large targeted group of people to connect with. Next, add yourself to this circle and share it. Now when users click *Add People,* they will add the original group plus you, so you'll gain even more new followers.

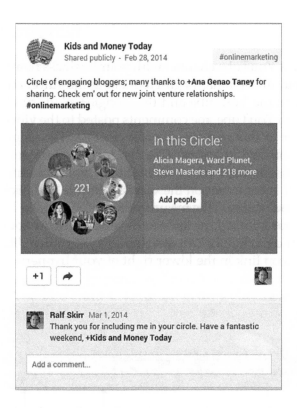

The image above has a circle of 221 people. If you were to click the *Add People* button, you would add 221 people to your circle (you would be following these 221 people). If you add yourself to this circle, it will contain 222 people when you share it.

Circle shares are just another post, so anyone can comment on them. The person above who said, "Thank you..." has highlighted himself from the group. His image is shown, and his name is linked back to his Profile. Commenting gives you more exposure.

You should eventually go through and look at these 221 profiles and perhaps, split them into more targeted circles. People will be doing the same with you — reviewing your Profile, so make sure your Profile indicates a reason people should circle you.

Here are some hashtags you might use to find shared circles and also include when you share circles yourself:

#circles #circleshare #sharedcircle #circlesharing #followers #circlecount #sharedcircles #sharedpubliccircles #circleshared #sharedcircleoftheday #addmetoyourcircles #awesomepeople #newfollowers #googleplus #social

LinkedIn

Establish your profile on LinkedIn using your own name (not your business name). After you grow your Profile strength, you might eventually qualify to open a company page.

When you are working on your Profile, you should turn off your activity broadcasts at *Settings > Profile > Turn on/off*, so you don't send excessive notifications to your connections.

LinkedIn has a reputation as a business-to-business networking site. It's for people looking for jobs, offering jobs, and connecting for joint ventures. It has never really been viewed as a site to sell products, but you should still have a presence there because you don't know what the future holds for you. (Freelance work?)

LinkedIn should be treated as another search engine. You find your connections, and they find you, through keywords used in profile tag lines, current job title, past title, skills, and summary.

As always, completely fill out all options in your profile. Use keywords in your description and job title. Most Profiles look like resumes, so try to make yours distinct. You can drag and drop Profile items to different locations on the page or add a video. You might tweak your summary to state your solution to a problem — give the viewer a reason to contact you.

Gaining followers may be more difficult than on other networks. LinkedIn was designed to connect with people you *already* knew and you're supposed to have them introduce you to new contacts.

You can see the last 5 people who looked at your profile. You might begin by attempting to connect with them. They've already shown an interest in your since they visited your page.

When you search LinkedIn, the results you see are based on your connections which includes your friends, their friends, and extended friends (friends of friends). The larger your network, the more extensive your *reach*. Many people have a strict LinkedIn policy of only connecting with people they actually know, but when you think about "reach potential," you might decide to have a more permissive policy. What might happen if you connect to someone with a reach of 10,000 people?

Lastly, check your privacy settings. Some people hide their connections. Will you allow other people to see that you looked at their profile? As we discussed above, this is another way to let people see you and you gain exposure. You might want to lighten up on some of your privacy choices.

Introduction to List Building

Offline Networking

Zazzle is an online business that you can work from home, but you might also look into marketing offline. Working from home can get lonely. Networking helps you make friends. Networking can also help boost your online business. Look for anything from local business meetings to clubs to athletic groups. You can network and share ideas while playing golf, eating dinner, or exercising with a friend. You might show off some products: wear a Zazzle shirt or leggings, carry a bag, or show off an iPhone case.

When you attend meetings, swap business cards. These should be your next purchase after your Domain name. Add your photo to the back of the card to help people remember you. Use the same photo displayed on your LinkedIn and Google+ Profile.

Even if you don't have your own cards yet, you can still collect business cards from others. Take these cards and visit each of your social networks to search for this person. Add them to your network. Place them in a group that helps you remember where you met them or in a group based on *your* target audience. What do you sell that this person might be interested in? Are they someone who you might do a joint promotion with? Place them in a group called "joint ventures." You can put them in two groups if necessary. Every social network is a form of list building.

While you attend networking meetings, listen carefully and ask yourself how you can do what the other attendees are doing—but do it in your business model. Not everything offline correlates to something online but often you can revise it a little to make it fit.

> *Example:* A common tip shared at networking meetings is to send a handwritten thank-you card to a customer or business partner. It's so uncommon these days, that it makes you stand out from the crowd. You could modify this. Send a note from Zazzle. It wouldn't be handwritten, but you can still personalize it with text and it still comes in the mail in a box—and bulky mail gets attention. Plus, you are able to show off your design.

Take fifteen minutes after every networking meeting and write down three action items that you can do immediately and just one or two that you might do in the long run. This keeps you from taking too many notes. You don't want to be a good note-taker; you want to grow your business by taking action.

Send a thank-you email to each networking acquaintance and invite them to opt-in to your list. Try something short like:

> "It was nice to meet you at (event name). You gave me some great ideas on (topic). You sounded interested in (benefit your newsletter provides). If you would like to keep in touch, please sign up for my newsletter at (opt-in link)."

Meetup

To find your local groups and organizations, try word of mouth. Ask at your church, child's school, or any other place you frequent to see what others recommend. Be careful about groups that charge fees. We suggest you browse http://Meetup.com. They describe their site as:

> "Meetup is the world's largest network of local groups. Meetup makes it easy for anyone to organize a local group or find one of the thousands already meeting up face-to-face. More than 9,000 groups get together in local communities each day, each one with the goal of improving themselves or their communities."

You can search by location and interest topics to find groups in your area. You might eventually begin your own group, but there is an annual fee and it requires a lot of time, so it's best to wait until you have some steady Zazzle income. Instead, attend other people's meetings. You get all the benefits, with very little work.

Occasionally in this book, we mention something like "You may need to ask someone for help." You can find these people at networking meetings. Look for more than your targeted buying audience. Find someone who knows about computer repair, taxes, coding, Search Engine Optimization, WordPress, local advertising, etc. and grow your network of resources, a contact list.

You might also find income opportunities at these meetings. Consider freelance work. Do these people need a customized item for each attendee of their own event? Design it for them.

MailChimp

It's never too early to begin building a list of interested targeted customers. MailChimp is a free list building service found online. If you use our link to sign up and ever decide to upgrade to a paid plan, we would receive a small affiliate commission, so, please consider using this link to join:

http://KidsandMoneyToday.com/mailchimp/

After creating your account, your main goal is to obtain a URL link for people to opt-in to your list. There will be many fun fancy features such as designing a customized newsletter, but ignore this for now. We just want to get your URL to add to your social media networks, blog, business cards, and products. (We will also suggest a minor change to a default form.)

This is only general MailChimp guidance. They have numerous tutorials on the site if you want to delve deeper. Eventually, you should customize your forms with your branding, and consider upgrading to a paid plan so you can use their autoresponder feature. Autoresponders are emails automatically sent to lead your subscribers down a specific path toward a sale. At the start though, you only need an opt-in URL, so we'll help you with that.

This is not a step-by-step screenshot tutorial, but we've included some screens to assist you.

Immediately after you create a new list, you should receive a confirmation note that includes a link to Customize your list. Click that to get started:

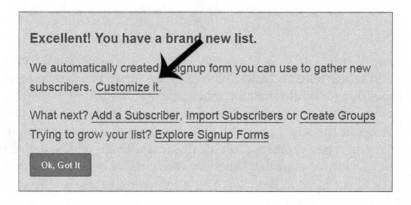

When you click the *Customize it* link, you'll be taken to the *Create Forms* page. If you click the drop-down menu next to the *Signup form,* you will notice there are numerous types of forms. There are so many that there is a scroll bar to reach the bottom of the list! At the moment, you only need to edit the forms we discuss.

Signup Form: Click to open the *Signup Form.* Eventually you should return here and add a banner to this form. Your embedded banner image should match your custom banner (discussed later) that you will create for your Zazzle store. You do not have to use a banner at the start. This will slow you down, so just complete the required basic information for this form. There will be a place to add a Title for your list. When you enter this, keep in mind that this field is visible to the user. You might want to use a Title that contains your brand name.

Signup Thank You Page: The *Thank You Page* is what your users will see in their browser immediately after they click *subscribe*. Since you are guaranteed that users will see this page, you should optimize it by giving them a *call to action*, something to do.

The default setting tells the user to check their email. Instead, you might edit this to invite subscribers to "Like" your Facebook Page. Below is an example of such an edit. You can see we replaced the "Almost finished..." box with an edited "Confirm" message and added a link to "Like us on Facebook" in the second box.

My Test Newsletter

Almost finished...

We need to confirm your email address.

To complete the subscription process, please click the link in the email we just sent you.

|HTML:LIST_ADDRESS_HTML|

« return to our website

Before

My Test Newsletter

To Confirm Your Subscription:

Click the link in the email we just sent you.

Here's what you can do now:

Click to Like us on Facebook

|HTML:LIST_ADDRESS_HTML|

« return to our website

After

Use the edit settings to optimize your own *Thank You Page*. To create the Facebook link in the lower box:

• Type "Here's what you can do now: " and "Click to Like us on Facebook." Select the "Like us on Facebook" text with your cursor, and click the *link icon* in your editor menu.

• In the pop-up window, copy in your full Facebook Page URL: http://facebook.com/YourPageName. Then, close it.

You can add a link to any form. We've got you started by setting up a link to "Like" your Facebook page. When you have more time, come back and consider adding your banner to *all* your forms and possibly adding links to other social networks or even to unique pages in your Zazzle store. Customize your *Unsubscribe* pages too. Entice them to stay. What might you tell them before they leave?

Begin paying attention to the forms and emails that you receive when you opt-in to other sites. Swipe the ideas that you like and add them to your own forms.

MailChimp has an App to place a Subscribe tab on your Facebook page. Click on *Signup forms,* then click the *Facebook form* option to get started.

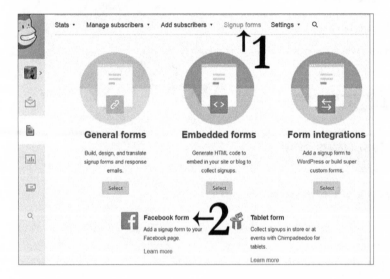

Follow the instructions provided by MailChimp to add this tab to your Facebook Page. The end result looks like this:

We came to MailChimp to get your opt-in URL to build your list of interested targeted customers. You'll find this URL back on the *Create Forms* page. To go back there, click the left navigation *Lists icon*, choose your list, and click *Signup Forms* > *General Forms* (You can see this option in the prior image, under the first large circle.) After clicking, you will see your URL located below the *Signup Form* drop-down menu.

Copy this URL in a browser to see how the live form looks on a page. Sign up for your own list and review the entire process: the emails the user receives and the screens that appear in the browser. Make changes as desired.

When you are happy with your basic setup, you can now add your MailChimp Opt-in URL to:

1. Your email signature.

2. Your business cards.

3. Pinterest descriptions of your own Zazzle items.

4. Your YouTube channel in both the description and as an active link in your banner.

5. Twitter: You have two locations for links in your Profile. Use one for your store; use the other for your opt-in page.

6. A monthly post scheduled on each social media site to capture new followers from the last thirty days.

7. The back of Zazzle products, such as note cards.

8. All pages of your blog.

Note: Don't let anyone tell you that MailChimp cannot be used for affiliate links. Read their policy here:
http://kb.mailchimp.com/article/does-mailchimp-ban-affiliate-links

Branding

Optimize your store at *My Account> Store > About Page.* Check *Enable This About Page,* and *Show Latest Products Created.* You might also check *Show Latest Products Sold.* Type in your store description with keywords. Include your opt-in URL with a note for the user to copy and paste the URL, since html is not permitted.

In the left menu, click *Settings* and complete your store title and tags. Next, click *Social Networking* to add your social media URLs.

Your Products

You can use your products as advertising tools. Copy ideas from cards you've purchased or received. As you browse ads in magazines or see how people post images on Pinterest, you might think of new ideas to brand your business.

The image below is the reverse side of a greeting card. It contains a miniature image matching the image on the front and has the Zazzle store URL beneath it. The recipient might turn this card over and visit the store. This is easy free advertising.

The back of this card could also have contained four mini images of unique products, or the URL could have been a link to an opt-in newsletter. Zazzle doesn't yet provide a way for us to collect customer information, so this might be a strategy to subtly ask for it on your own.

Understanding Your Income

Before you begin creating products, you'll want to have a general understanding of how much you'll be paid. You wouldn't want to spend significant time designing and promoting and then realize the income wasn't worth your effort. As noted earlier, you can earn money on Zazzle by either designing products for sale or by referring other buyers to Zazzle.

This chapter explains your income from each of these types of earnings and explains in detail the following terms:

- *Referral, Referral Commission, or Associate Commission:* Earnings from a product you help sell; your role is the referrer.

- *Royalty or Royalty Rate:* Earnings from a design you license for sale on a product; your role is the designer.

- *Self-Referred Sale:* A sale of your design on a product that came through your referral. Your role is both the designer and referrer.

- *3rd Party Sale:* A sale of your design on a product that occurs as a result of someone else's referral. Your role is the designer.

- *Referral Fee:* A fee you pay when your sold product was referred, whether the referral was by you or someone else. Your role is the designer; the designer pays this fee.

Your earnings appear in two reports: your *Referral Report* and your *Royalty Report*.

- *Referral Report:* Displays products sold (including your own) through your referrals, the product price, and your 15% associate commission earned.

- *Royalty History Report:* Displays products sold with your design and the royalties paid. This report also indicates:

  — Referral sales: Indicated by None, 3rd Party, or Self

  — Customization: Indicated by "c" when a product has been customized (such as adding additional text or images)

Sales from Referrals

Associate referral commissions are a little easier to understand than royalties, so we'll discuss these types of earnings first. Associates use the terms "commission," "earned referral," or simply "referral" to describe these types of sales. When you use your Associate ID to refer customers to Zazzle and they make a purchase, you earn a 15% *referral commission*.

You can earn referrals by referring your own or other store owner's items.

> *Example:* You like a mug sold by another store owner and decide to share it on Facebook. If a buyer enters Zazzle using your link and purchases the mug (or any other item), Zazzle will pay you a *referral commission* of 15% of the sale price.

Always use your Associate ID when making a Zazzle purchase, including when you purchase your own designs on products. This ensures you earn your 15% referral commission. Some sellers bookmark their referral URL in their browser so they can click quickly and rest assured that their Associate ID is set.

We suggest you always double check your referral purchases. After completing the purchase, view your Referral Report and if you don't see the referral, then for whatever reason, the tracking ID did not record. If checked immediately, you will have time to cancel your order and repurchase.

Volume Sales Bonus

The Volume Sales Bonus is one reason this book has a heavy focus on the associate side of Zazzle. You earn a Monthly Volume Sales Bonus for qualifying referral sales, defined as:

> "Qualifying subtotals of referrals within a user's account, minus any earnings that were awarded for the referral."

These referrals must take place on the same Zazzle site. This means, although your created items automatically appear on all Zazzle sites, including Zazzle's international sites using different URL endings (such as http://Zazzle.ca), your volume sales bonus is *not calculated* from the sum of sales across all sites.

If you are interested in a bonus, you must think beyond product creation and develop a plan to bring buyers into the marketplace. The sales bonus award rates for qualifying referral sales are:

- 0% Bonus (Level 1): Sales between $0.00 – 99.99
- 1% Bonus (Level 2): Sales between $100.00 – 999.99
- 5% Bonus (Level 3): Sales between $1,000.00 – 5,199.99
- 12% Bonus (Level 4): Sales between $5,200.00 – $99,999.99
- 17% Bonus (Level 5): Sales between $100,000 and above

The lowest level is not that difficult to earn. The 1% bonus is achieved at just $100 in qualifying referral sales. But, a 1% bonus on $100 is only $1, so this is not too much to get excited about. However, it may make you feel good and you might feel motivated to keep trying to reach higher levels. It's challenging, but not impossible, to reach these levels. Your potential to reach higher levels should increase by using strategies in this book.

Sales from Your Designs

When you design products for sale, you have the potential to earn royalties. A Royalty is the amount of money paid for the use of something.

> *Example:* Authors receive royalties from a publisher. The publisher pays for the right to sell the work, the writing, which is owned by the author. Zazzle is also a publisher. Zazzle prints your designs on products and pays you a royalty each time your design is used on products sold.

When you hear something is "Royalty Free," or has a "Royalty Free license," this means the person with the rights to the item (book, design, music, etc.) will allow it to be used without paying royalties back to the author, artist, or musician.

There can still be an initial cost. You could sell your design for a one-time fee of $500 along with a Royalty Free license. This means you would receive $500 and the recipient would not have to pay you any future royalties when your design is used.

Understanding the different types of "use" licenses is important because while some designers create their own original designs, others purchase Royalty Free images and mistakenly think the image can be used legally on Zazzle products. However, a Royalty Free license, for example, is not a "Commercial Use" license. It does not give you permission to sell, so designers must read further to determine if commercial use is permitted.

> *Example:* If you buy a song, it is royalty free because you don't have to pay the musician every time you use (listen to) it, but you don't own a Commercial Use license for that song. It would be illegal for you to sell the song.

Another option is to sell your design for $500 with a Royalty Free and "Editorial license." Here too, you would not be paid any future royalties, but you have given the recipient permission to use your design in an editorial piece, like a newspaper. You have not given commercial rights to sell or make a profit using your design as commercial rights require a Commercial Use license.

Royalties can be a flat rate, such as authors who might receive ten cents for every book sold, or a percentage of the sale. On Zazzle, royalties are computed as a percentage, and you can choose your percentage rate. This is called your *royalty rate*. In most cases, your royalty is calculated based on the sales price. (One exception is postage stamps where your royalty is calculated on the "mark-up" of the price printed on the stamp.)

Setting your Royalty Rate is difficult. The challenge is figuring out the highest price to sell your item, without losing the sale. Don't be afraid to test higher rates. You can set some items below 15% and others above. If you select a group of items by category or product type, you can bulk edit the entire group. Your royalty changes will take place on or around the 20th of every month.

In the end, your goal will be to sell in a quantity that you consider successful. For many artists, income is not always the overruling factor. Some artists feel their work should demand a certain minimum price. These artists would feel devalued if their items sold for any less. They will not care if you point out that they might sell more at a lower price, and thus, net a higher income.

In the end, personal feelings and pride usually play a hidden role in setting royalty rates. There's no "best percentage" to use. Each seller's choice will be different, so you'll have to determine a rate that's acceptable for you.

While your Royalty Rate sets your initial income expectations, other factors may impact your actual take-home pay. These include: transaction fees, customization, promotions, minor adjustments to royalty rates, and referral fees (all discussed next).

Transaction Fee

Zazzle charges a 5% transaction fee for a royalty rate set at 15% or higher. The transaction fee is calculated off of your royalty amount, not the sales price.

> *Example:* You sell a $20 item set at 30% royalty. Your initial royalty is $6.00 ($20 sale price × 30%), but instead you'll receive $5.70 ($6.00 - ($6.00 × 5% transaction fee)).

If you are thinking of setting a royalty near 15%, you should choose a 14.9% royalty rate. By doing this, you avoid the extra fee and come out ahead with more money in your pocket.

> *Example:* You have a $20 item. If you sell it at 15% royalty, you'll receive $2.85 ($3 initial royalty - ($3 × 5% transaction fee)). Sell it at the lower 14.9% royalty and you'll receive $2.98 ($20 × 14.9%).

Customization Bonus

When you see a tiny little 'c' in your Royalty Report, this indicates a design has been customized.

Some customization can increase your income, such as if a buyer were to purchase a framed print, as opposed to the print alone. Zazzle states:

> "We will pay you a 5% fixed royalty on specialty options and add-ons such as printing on additional design areas, 2XL and up sizes, and print frames."

To increase your opportunities for higher sales, you might always allow your items to be customized. This option appears when you post your items for sale. The pros and cons of customization are discussed more later, in the Create Products chapter.

Zazzle Promotions

Some store owners set their royalty below 15% to be eligible for Zazzle promotions. Zazzle defines promotions as special offers on "select" items or appearing on Zazzle's list of featured products, home page, newsletter, email campaigns, blog, Groupon.com deals, or collection pages (such as the wedding collections page).

Here are some things to consider about Zazzle promotions when deciding on your Royalty Rate:

- *No Guarantee of Promotion:* Just because you set your royalty under 15%, there is no guarantee that your item will ever be chosen for promotion.

- *Perceived Inequity:* Someone who refers your product earns a 15% commission. If your Royalty Rate is under 15%, the person making the referral will earn more than you. As the designer, are you comfortable with this idea?

- *Site-wide Coupon Eligibility:* When your royalty is set at 15% or higher, your items are still eligible for Zazzle's site-wide coupons. A high royalty rate does not exclude your products from all discount offers.

- *Coupon Impact on Income:* You will feel the impact of coupons. Your Royalty Report will show less than you've received in the past. When you expected to receive $8 for an item and it sells at 75% discount—earning you only $2, how will you feel? You might nudge your Royalty Rate higher to withstand these discount-type promotions and to ensure you are satisfied when coupons are used.

Sometimes, promotions help you fine tune your royalty rates. If you have an item that surges in sales during a promotion, this might indicate that you have set your royalty too high.

> *Example:* Your current royalty rate earns you $2 per sale. You usually sell to 5 customers per month, netting you $10 ($2 x 5 buyers). During a 50% off sale, you sell 100 items, netting you $100 ($2 x 50% x 100 buyers). You might test reducing your royalty rate, to see if this quantity will continue to sell on a regular basis. $100 a month is better than $10.

If the demand for an item significantly increases at a lower price, you can net a higher monthly income.

Adjusting Your Royalty Rate for Extra Pennies

The royalty rate calculator appears when you create items, after your click *Post for Sale*. It's in the section titled *Royalty Information*, below your title, description, and tags and looks like this:

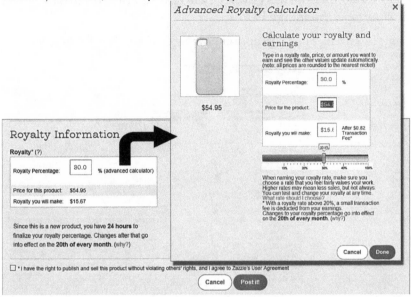

Use this calculator to maximize your royalty without changing the customer price. Begin by entering a royalty rate that gives you a reasonable price for your product. Next, slowly nudge up the royalty rate (percentage) until you see the sales price change. Set your royalty to the percentage just prior to the sales price change.

> *Example:* You choose a 30% royalty on a $54.95 item to earn you a $15.67 profit. You nudge the royalty upward and find that at 31% the sales price changes, so you set your royalty to 30.9%. The customer's price remains the same at $54.95, yet you increased your take-home pay by .46; you earn $16.13 verses $15.67. Conveniently, the calculator will recognize royalties set at 15% or higher and automatically deduct the 5% transaction fee.

Royalty Rate	Sales Price	Less 5% Transaction Fee	Profit
30.0%	$54.95	- (30.0% × $54.95)× 5%	$15.67
30.4%	$54.95	- (30.4% × $54.95)× 5%	$15.86
30.8%	$54.95	- (30.8% × $54.95)× 5%	$16.07
30.9%	*$54.95*	*- (30.9% × $54.95)× 5%*	*$16.13*
31%	$55.95	- (31.0% × $54.95)× 5%	$16.47

Referral Fees Reduce Your Royalty

Your royalty will always be reduced 20% on all your sales that have been referred. Your Royalty Report shows whether your sales were not referred (None), Self-referred or 3rd Party referred as shown in the image below:

Sample *Royalty History* Report showing Self and 3rd Party sales.

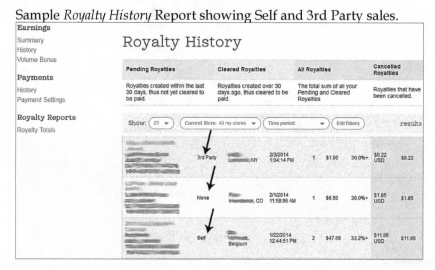

This fee contributes toward all the back-end requirements for referred sales. Store owners do not have to interact with the associates. You don't handle questions, track any clicks a buyer made, provide reports to associates, or issue commission checks. Zazzle does all of this for you, and in exchange, charges you, the seller, a *referral fee* calculated at 20% of your royalty amount.

You pay this referral fee regardless of whether you or someone else referred your product. Here are some examples to clarify this:

1. *You Share Your Product (You Earn Reduced Royalty & a Referral):* If you share *your watch* to Facebook and someone buys it, this is a self-referred sale. You are paid for your role as the designer and the sale appears in your Royalty Report. You pay a referral fee and receive a reduced royalty. Since you are also the referrer of your own product, you earn your 15% referral commission.

2. *Someone Shares Your Product (You Earn Reduced Royalty):* If someone else shares *your watch* to Facebook and someone buys it, this is a 3rd party referral sale. You are paid for your role as the designer and the sale appears in your Royalty Report. You pay a referral fee and receive a reduced royalty.

3. *You Share Someone Else's Product (You Earn a Referral):* If you share *someone else's* watch to Facebook and someone buys it, the *designer* of this watch has the 3rd party referral sale in his or her Royalty Report and the designer pays the referral fee. This is not a Royalty Sale for you. Your role in this sale is as an Associate, so your *Referral Report* reflects the sale you made—a sale of a product that was not yours (indicated by "No" in the image below) and you earn a 15% referral commission.

Sample *Referral Report* - A referral of someone else's product:

	Product	My Product?	Date	Subtotal	Rate	Referral	Referral (USD)
Referral Reports		No	3/23/2014 9:08:46 AM	$54.52	15%	$8.18 USD	$8.18

In the first two cases your royalty is reduced by the referral fee, because you designed the item sold through a referral. In the first and third case, you receive a 15% referral commission, because in both these cases, you acted as an Associate for Zazzle.

Computing the 20% Referral Fee

The easiest and most useful way to compute the 20% referral fee is to calculate the fee from your initial royalty figure.

You calculate your initial royalty from the sales price. Next, your referral fee is calculated based on this initial royalty amount and then you subtract the fee from your royalty.

> *Example:* Your Royalty History Report shows a $20 referral sale and your royalty is set at 14.9%. It does not matter if the sale is 3rd Party or Self-referred. The royalty is computed as follows:
>
> $2.98 initial royalty ($20 × 14.9%)
> -$ .596 ($2.98 × 20% referral fee)
> $2.38 royalty received

Calculating it this way makes it easy to see that the store owner pays only $ .596 toward the expenses related to the associate sale. Without a referral, you would have earned $2.98 ($20 × 14.9%), but instead, you receive $2.38.

Also remember that if this was a Self-referred sale, you would also earn a 15% referral commission and net $5.38:

$2.38 Royalty previously calculated
+ $3.00 Referral commission ($20 sale price × 15% associate rate)
$5.38

This is why we recommend to always use your referral URL when making purchases, even for your own products.

Also recall that if your royalty is set greater than 15%, you will incur the additional 5% transaction fee. Your royalty is then reduced by 25% (the 20% referral fee + the 5% transaction fee).

> *Example:* Your Royalty History Report shows a $20 referral sale and your royalty is set at 30%. It does not matter if the sale is 3rd Party or Self-referred. The royalty is computed as follows:
>
> $6.00 Initial royalty($20 × 30% Royalty Rate)
> -$1.20 ($6 × 20% Referral fee)
> -$ .30 ($6 × 5% Transaction fee)
> $4.50 Royalty received

These formulas can be further simplified as shown below:

Under 15% Royalty:
No Referral: Royalty = Sales Price × Royalty Rate
Referral: Royalty = Sales Price × Royalty Rate × 80%

Royalty set at 15% or higher:
No Referral: Royalty = Sales Price × Royalty Rate × 95%
Referral: Royalty = Sales Price × Royalty Rate × 75%

Zazzle provides royalty details at:
http://Zazzle.com/sell/designers/nameyourroyalty/

Create Products

It's worth repeating, the most common mistake we see small businesses owners make—everywhere, not just in Print on Demand—is thinking about their business in the wrong order. Many business owners think, "I like this, so I will create it, sell it, and make money." Sometimes this works, but more often, it doesn't. A more profitable approach is to say, "I see a demand for this, so I will create it, sell it, and make money."

When you learn what people are looking for and create that, your chances of making a sale are much better. So before you begin creating products, you might revisit your notes on target audience and reconsider how your customer will find you. This chapter will discuss strategies that help buyers find your products.

Optimization

Optimization refers to the steps you take to get something found. We optimize our Internet pages to be found in search engines. We optimize our social media posts so they can be found on social media. On Zazzle, we will optimize our products so they rank well on both Zazzle and in search engines. All pages, your product and store pages (home, category, and product type pages) can rank in search engine results.

Search Engine Optimization (SEO) refers to steps you can take to make your website rank higher in search engines. The same techniques used for SEO should also help your items rank well within the Zazzle marketplace and your posts rank well on social networks. Factors impacting ranking are: keywords, links, views, price, sales, age, and shares to social media.

When you create items on Zazzle, you begin on the Product Creation screen. This is where you can add images and text, re-size these additions to fit nicely, and choose your options (such as round, square, background color, etc.). After you're satisfied with your design, click *Post for Sale* and a screen will appear to add information about your design. This is where you will begin to optimize your design to rank well. This is the screen you should think about before you even begin to create a design, because this is how a customer will find you.

Post for Sale **screen:**

Post Product for Sale

Describe and organize your product so that other people can find it!

Please note that it can take up to 24 hours for your product to appear in search results.

(* required field)

Title and Description

Title *
Try to describe your item the way a shopper would.

Description *
Tell the item's story and add security to spaces!

(Html, HTML, is incomplete here!)

Categories

Choose **at least one** of the following: *

Category (Select)

(none selected)
Select a category that describes your design or content.

Events & Occasions (Select)

(none selected)
Select an event or occasion that your product is meant for.

Recipient (Select)

(none selected)
Select a suitable recipient for your product.

Have an idea about a new category? Tell us about it.

Store Category 1 (Change | Clear) *

tracytrends ▼

> Sunflowers

Tags *

[   ] (Add Tag(s))

View tags above as text | Remove all tags above

☑ Power Tags (0 of 10 used) (what's this?) | All Tags (0 of 40 used) | Characters (0 of 600 used)

Additional Information

Suitable Audience* (?)

| G | PG-13 | R |
| ◉ | ○ | ○ |

Product Visibility* (?)
○ Public (everyone can see it) ◉ Hidden (only you can see it) ○ Direct-only

Make product a template? (?)
◉ Yes ○ No

Show "Customize it" button?(?)
◉ Yes ○ No

Royalty Information

Royalty* (?)

Royalty Percentage:	30.0	% (advanced calculator)
Price for this product:	$2.45	
Royalty you will make:	$0.70	

Since this is a new product, you have **24 hours** to finalize your royalty percentage. Changes after that go into effect on the **20th of every month**. (why?)

☐ * I have the right to publish and sell this product without violating others' rights, and I agree to Zazzle's User Agree

(Cancel) (Post It!)

Keep in mind that Zazzle (just like Google) keeps their algorithm a secret. No one knows for sure what impacts ranking. The items discussed next are speculation based on our own experience and ideas shared in the forums.

Keywords

Keywords are the core of how information is found online. If we create a beautiful cat poster and never use the word *cat* anywhere, under normal circumstances, that item will not be found in search for *cat*. Algorithms are kept secret but, the fact is they work by reading words (along with other indicators).

Your first step is to focus on these words, referred to as your *keywords*. You will use these keywords when posting your products for sale. Use your ideas from the research you did earlier, when we discussed target audience. You'll want to have keywords for your store as a whole, keywords for categories, and keywords for designs. You may repeat words in each location.

Visit the Zazzle marketplace. Put yourself in the shoes of your customers. What will they type in the search box to find your item? If you don't know what to type — that's a lesson in itself. You might backtrack a little and think about your target audience. Who are you trying to reach? What are they looking for? You want to be able to fill this need to make your sale. People make purchases to solve things. What does your product solve? All these ideas might help you discover keywords to use.

Look for trending topics. Look for questions people type into search engines, such as "How to throw a baby shower?" or a phrase that could apply to a Zazzle product, such as "Baby Gift." You might create customizable invitations, pacifiers, or baby blankets using these keywords. Try to focus on *buying keywords*. Words like "Best Wedding Favor" could mean a person is still researching, but "Wedding Favors under $25" might indicate a person ready to purchase. The words people type in search can help tell you what to create on Zazzle. This is what we mean by finding the demand for a product — before you create it.

Keywords can be especially difficult for the abstract graphic designers. When you have a swirl of multiple colors, you'll have to brainstorm or research to find the right words that ensure your item will show for your targeted customer.

There are many free Internet tools to help you find keywords. We've listed some in the Resource section in the back of this book.

Competition

When you have your keywords, check the marketplace for your volume of competition. Type in your words and see how many items are currently listed. There are 36,436 results for *New York City*. If you want to create something with an image of New York City, your keywords will need to be much more specific. You don't want to compete against 36,436 items for the first spot in the marketplace results. Initially, it will be difficult to rank against that level of competition. Instead, try to rank for a longer phrase and after ranking well for that, adjust to compete for shorter terms.

You might choose *New York City Sunset* with only about 625 results. You might narrow it down even further, by product type. Perhaps you want to compete in the mug or sticker section.

This is only the first part of research. There might be only 625 results because there is no demand for a product with *New York City Sunset*. At this point, you will have to make a choice. You can research further. Or, you might research by testing, which means, go ahead and create the design. If it sells, you'll know you're on to something and should create similar items.

One way to research further is to use Google Adwords. You will have to look for some tutorials on the Internet to teach you how to use this. The basic idea is that you can use Adwords to see what words are demanding high bids and for how long. Companies will not pay for ads that do not perform, so if a company continues to pay a high price for a keyword, then the income generated by that word must exceed the advertising price. If the company pays $1 for an ad and the ad generates $2, then the company is always ahead and will continue placing the ad. Adwords can help you discover new keywords to use for your products and can help you identify a demand before you begin creating.

Another place to do research is browsing the marketplace competition. Don't copy someone's exact design, but by viewing their item, you can get keyword ideas. Look at the words they used in their titles, description, and tags.

Don't ever use unrelated keywords, even if they are words that might help you rank well. These are not words that will bring you targeted buyers, and your goal is to generate sales.

To summarize, before creating your item, determine if there is a demand for your product, the amount of competition already in place, and what keywords you will use to help people find your items. This should result in faster sale conversions.

Post for Sale page - Title and Description:

```
                Post Product for Sale


Describe and organize your product so that other people can find it!

Please note that it can take up to 24 hours for your product to appear in search results.


                                                              ( * required field)

   Title and Description
   Title *
   Try to describe your item the way a shopper would.
   [                                                                    ]

   Description *
   Tell the item's story and explain why it's special.
   [                                                                    ]
   [                                                                    ]
   [                                                                   .:]

   (What HTML is acceptable here?)
```

Title

Titles can always help you rank higher. Titles are used on individual Zazzle items as shown above, but we also use titles in our store name, categories, social media posts, and blogs. The rules are the same, regardless of where your title is located.

Your title words should indicate what you are *relevant* for. All ranking algorithms are designed to rank by relevancy.

Order matters. Usually, words used first in a title are weighted more. Theoretically, a *Pet Loss - Sympathy Greeting Card,* should rank higher for a search of "Pet Loss Card" than a search for "Sympathy Card" because the words "Pet Loss" are listed first. Of course, it could rank well for both terms once other indicators are factored in.

The words you choose for your title not only help you to rank, but they grab the customer's attention. Titles are also pulled into RSS feeds by associates, and titles show in search engine results. When your customer sees the list of search results, you want the customer to read your title and feel a desire to click through.

You don't have to add the product type, such as mug, greeting card, and so forth to your title. Zazzle will attach this to your title automatically (although this can sometimes take 24 hours or more to appear, depending on when Zazzle runs updates).

Description

Your description should also use keywords. List your most important keywords used toward the beginning. Some sellers use the practice of immediately repeating the title at the beginning of their description. Others open with similar, related keywords, or synonyms.

As a general rule of thumb, we suggest you create a description as if you were describing your item to a blind person. You will find this helps you come up with many more words. Things like colors, emotions, and texture, could be added. Next, think of how your item might be used. This should give you more words. Keep your words targeted and not spammy. Save your list, because you might use these words in other marketing.

Consider using hashtags in your product descriptions. This might help exposure when items are posted to social media — assuming the hashtag carries through.

If you want more advanced descriptions, read the next section about creating links. Since your description can be updated at anytime, if you'd prefer to learn this topic later, you can skip ahead to *Categories*.

Links

You are permitted to use HTML in your product descriptions (although Zazzle has recently announced they may remove this). Since it is still active as of this writing, we've included some linking ideas for you.

Inbound links impact ranking. These are pages linking to your product page. They have the most impact when the link comes to your Zazzle page from a different website. You will have some of these links already, from posting your products to social media and blogs. Links within Zazzle, meaning a Zazzle page linking to another Zazzle page, count a little too, so this is one reason you might add some links in your product descriptions.

A second reason to add links is to offer the user other related options. If your description is short, your link will be visible on the product page. When you use longer descriptions, Zazzle adds a *read more* link in the description area and the user will have to click through to see your description link.

Description links may also encourage an associate to choose to promote your item. If you have a detailed item description, along with links to relevant products, you save associates time when they post your item to their blog. A lot of content is already there, so there is very little extra coding for the associate to do. Also, your description links will offer other options to entice a buyer to click through to Zazzle. This is good for the associate and can also help increase your views, which can help improve your ranking.

To add a clickable link to another product of yours on Zazzle, you might use the format below. Replace *itemURL* and *Item Title* with the product URL and title of the product you wish to link to:

<a href="itemURL">*Item Title*</a>

Just type this format into your description. A link to the Pet Loss card, mentioned above, looks like this:

<a href="http://zazzle.com/pet_loss_sympathy_greeting_card-137000542929671361">*Pet Loss - Sympathy Greeting Card*</a>

If you are trying to rank a specific item, you could create links to that item from all the descriptions of your *related and relevant* products to try and boost its ranking position.

Another linking strategy is to create a link that takes the user to a group of products. You can use this strategy to recommend matching products. If a user clicks through, it will bring you extra views and possibly sales.

You create this link by placing a unique tag in several products either in the descriptions (must be short descriptions so you don't trigger the *read more* feature) or as a power tag (in your first ten tags). Then, you create a link calling for this tag. When clicked, the link should pull all the products containing the tag. Use this format, but change *UniqueTag* to your tag:

<a href="http://zazzle.com/UniqueTag+gifts/">*More Items*</a>

Notice that we said, "should pull" a group of items. Zazzle has to find and index your unique tag for it to show in search results. Zazzle search is often buggy, meaning it doesn't always pull items as we think it should. Before using this type of link, load the URL in your browser to be sure it is pulling correctly.

An alternative option is to link to items grouped in Category pages, Wishlists, or Collections. These three methods of grouping are all discussed in detail later.

Categories

After clicking *Post for Sale*, in addition to your Title and Description boxes, you will choose your Category options. These include: *Category* (meaning the marketplace category), *Events & Occasions*, *Recipients*, and your store category.

Post for Sale page - Categories:

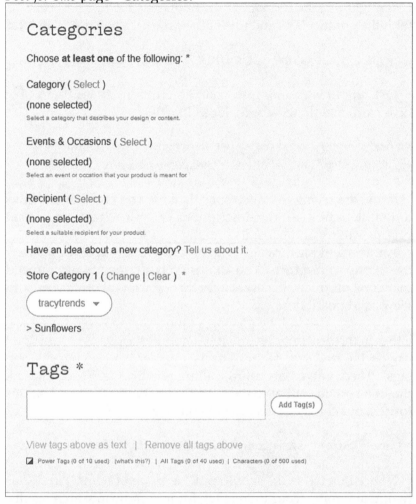

Sometimes your head begins to spin when you think about all the possible marketplace categories that could include your item. As a beginner, it's difficult to even imagine all the categories that Zazzle has even created.

When you are limited in time to do research, you can begin by placing your item in the same category chosen by the top ranking products. Visit the marketplace and enter your keywords in the Search box. Open a few products, scroll down each one and make a note of what categories the top ranking sellers are using. Pick the best match for your item.

When you have time to fine tune and consider new places for your item, take a look at the category tree Zazzle created in 2011. You can download the category tree file at:

http://zazzle.com/assets/graphics/z2/pub/zazzle_category_tree_v2.01.zip

It's a free download, and the structure looks like this:

Animals
Animals / Farm
Animals / Farm / Chickens
Animals / Farm / Chickens / Hens
Animals / Farm / Chickens / Roosters
Animals / Farm / Cows
Animals / Farm / Cows / Bulls
Animals / Farm / Donkeys & Mules
Animals / Farm / Ducks
Animals / Farm / Geese
Animals / Farm / Goats
Animals / Farm / Horses
Animals / Farm / Horses / Draft Horses

When you open this file, you can search for a term or just browse to find the best category for your item. From the grouping above you can see how if you had an item with a rooster design, this is a fast way to see what section to place it in. You might also use the category tree as a source to find new or related keywords.

You can always edit your marketplace category later. When you are creating items and pressed for time, you might just place your rooster in the *Animals* category, without drilling down through the extra clicks required to reach *Farm* and then *Chickens*. But at a later date, fine tuning this area might equate to more sales. It should also help in search results because your rooster should show in four categories: animals, farm, chickens, and roosters, which means you have four internal (within Zazzle) links to your product page.

Events & Occasions and Recipients

Many sellers don't worry about completing the *Events & Occasions* and *Recipient* area, maybe because it is not a required entry to post items for sale. However, their omission increases your opportunity to rank in these areas. Use everyone else's laziness to your advantage. Because there is less competition, your item may rank first for that customer who does drill down to lower levels. If you have the time, complete all options in the Categories section.

(There is currently no file, no tree type listing, to tell you all the *Events & Occasions* or *Recipient* options.)

Store Category Structure

Under the Category section, you will also choose where to place your item in your own store, your *store category* folder. So before you create an item, think about how your store structure relates to categories, events, and recipients.

You might use a mind mapping software to create an outline for your store. One software is XMind, a free download found at:
http://xmind.net/

Sample Store Structure

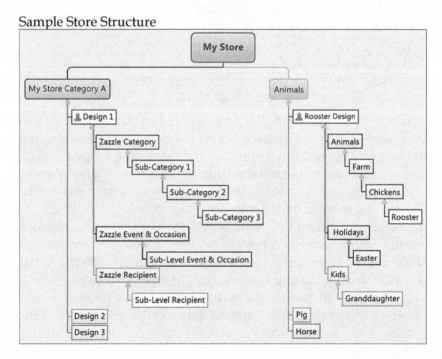

In the illustration, the left side of the mind map shows how your store category will contain your designs (Design 1, Design 2, Design 3). Then each design will be connected to a Zazzle *Category, Event/Occasion,* and *Recipient.* Additionally, each of these may or may not have their own sub-sections, as illustrated in the tiered format shown for Design 1. (Design 2 and Design 3 are not expanded out.)

Assuming our rooster design was an Easter card for a granddaughter, the right side shows a possible store structure.

When all options are completed, all products with this rooster design have the potential to show up in search results for:

- *Categories:* animals, farm, chickens, rooster
- *Events & Occasions:* holidays, Easter
- *Recipient:* kids, granddaughter

That's eight opportunities, not including our potential to rank for the keywords we enter in our title, description, and tags. This shows how drilling down to sub-sections can increase your chances for exposure and sales. You can also see a plan to expand the animal category to include Pig and Horse designs (entered in the respective Design 2 and Design 3 boxes).

Your store categories can be organized by design (like we did in the mind map with all products with the rooster design in one folder), or by department type (such as a folder containing all mugs, each with a different design), or a mixture of both options.

We prefer to organize by design for several reasons. The first is that your storefront already has a left menu navigation by department type, so visitors can use that to browse specific products.

Organizing by design also allows you to bulk edit groups of items very quickly. If you have 288 items containing the same image in one folder, you can select 96 at a time and change the title, descriptions, and tags with just a few clicks, and then, repeat the process.

No matter which method you choose, keep in mind that your category titles will create an additional left navigation menu on your storefront, so you will want to keep them short and easy to read. Use keywords and try not to change them once they are performing well, because these pages are indexed by search engines and will also appear in your Google analytic reports. It's hard to evaluate something if the name keeps changing.

Tags

Your first ten tags are *Power Tags* and these are the only tags that help your item rank in the Zazzle marketplace. All your tags will help your item rank in search engines.

You list your Zazzle tags by using commas between keywords and use a + sign or quotes to group a keyword phrase. For example, New+York+City and "New York City" both produce a tag phrase of *New York City*.

The tag limits are: 500 characters for all tags combined on one product, 40 tags total (ten of which are Power Tags), each tag must contain at least 3 characters, and phrases can use up to 5 words.

Choosing your Power Tags is often a challenge:

> *Example:* We have a card of a long stemmed red rose.
> Seller #1 uses: long, stemmed, red, rose, and six more tags.
> Seller #2 uses: "long stemmed red rose" and nine more tags.
> Seller #3 uses: "long stemmed red rose", "red rose", rose, and seven more tags.

When a buyer enters *long stemmed red rose* into the Zazzle search box, the marketplace would most likely rank seller #1 lower than the other two (all other factors being equal). This is because sellers #2 and #3 have indicated (by using the *exact phrase* in quotes) their item is *relevant*.

However, by listing words separately, you may increase your chance to be relevant for a mixture of terms and long-tail keyword phrases. Buyers will often narrow down their searches by adding an additional word to the end of their initial phrase. After viewing the results for *red rose,* a buyer might narrow the search by adding *long*. Seller #1 might rank best for the long-tail phrase of *red rose long* because Seller #1 listed each tag separately.

Since views also play a role in ranking, you might start by focusing on long-tail keywords and later, move tighter. Using the rose example, the search term *rose* produced 299,743 results on Zazzle, but the phrase *long stemmed red rose* had only 142 results. Initially, you might enter tags to rank on the first page for *"long stemmed red rose."* This will help you obtain additional views, because you'll be on page one. Next, adjust your tags and description to try and compete for *"red rose."* Change your tag order and phrases. You might also change your title and description.

After you appear on page one for *red rose*, consider competing for the term *rose* and make the necessary adjustments.

Of course, this all depends on what your competition is doing. If they are also increasing their views or making sales (which impacts ranking even more), then your rank may not change.

See more about tags at:

http://Zazzle.com/sell/designers/tutorials/tagging

http://forum.zazzle.com/create/why_tag_spam_hurts

Additional Information

After clicking *Post for Sale*, below the *Title and Description* and *Categories* sections, you will find the *Additional Information* section:

Post for Sale page - Additional Information:

Additional Information

Suitable Audience* (?)

G	PG-13	R
⦿	○	○

Product Visibility* (?)
○ Public (everyone can see it)   ⦿ Hidden (only you can see it)   ○ Direct-only

Make product a template? (?)
⦿ Yes ○ No

Show "Customize it" button?(?)
⦿ Yes ○ No

Royalty Information

Royalty* (?)

Royalty Percentage:	30.0	% (advanced calculator)
Price for this product:	$2.45	
Royalty you will make:	$0.70	

Since this is a new product, you have **24 hours** to finalize your royalty percentage. Changes after that go into effect on the **20th of every month**. (why?)

☐ * I have the right to publish and sell this product without violating others' rights, and I agree to Zazzle's User Agreement

(Cancel) (Post it!)

Visibility

Your choices for visibility are *Public, Hidden,* and *Direct Only*. Direct Only means the product will not be visible in the Zazzle Marketplace, any Store, or within any RSS feed. It can only be reached through external links or API integrations. This option is typically used by more advanced users who prefer to have a store on their own domain. It is also used for those who do freelance work and create customized items. You should also use this setting when you are ready to delete an item. Set it as *Direct Only* to be sure no one (such as an associate) is linking to it. After a month or two, if it has not received any new views, you can be fairly sure no one is linking to it and then, delete it.

Hidden Category

Categories can also be set to *hidden*. This means the category and items within it will not be visible to a user who views your *store pages*. However, it does not override the settings of the individual items placed inside the category. If you have unhidden products within a hidden category, these items *will show* up in the market-place search results.

Sellers use this set up for items that seem to clutter a store. They can reduce the quantity, reduce the clutter, seen by a store visitor but keep everything available for the marketplace search results.

> *Example*: Suppose you've placed your design on every possible style of Christmas ornament. None of the products are set to hidden. You might place all but one ornament in a *hidden category*. This means someone visiting your store would only see one ornament, yet all of them are available to rank in the marketplace results.

Private Store

You can also hide an entire storefront by setting it to *Private*. Go to *My Account* > *Store* > *Manage* > *Edit Settings* and under *Title,* check the *Make this store private* box.

Similar to hidden categories, a Private Store only means that you have no storefront for customers. Your items will still appear in the marketplace unless you set the item itself to Hidden or Direct Only.

Customization

Here's a list of reasons why some sellers choose *not to permit* customization of their products:

- I don't want someone altering my original design.

- I worry that the buyer will change my design in a manner that will reflect poorly on my business, poorly on me.

- The buyer could make changes and pass the item off as their own design, maybe reselling it at a local fair, etc.

- If I make a calendar of 12 images and they replace one with their own, the item no longer represents my original work. I don't want people mixing their designs with mine.

These are all valid concerns. However, visitors go to Zazzle because they want a *personalized* item. With customization off, you may be losing some significant income opportunities.

Age

Age refers to how *fresh* your item is. All search algorithms seem to use freshness as a ranking factor. They give weight to new, fresh content so it's much better to be creating products on a regular basis, than to create only once in a while. You can refresh older items by editing their description or change their Zazzle category.

Ironically, age also refers how long your item has been online. It's believed that some algorithms treat an older post like a wise old man. They've been around for a while. They are trustworthy, especially if they have click throughs, views, and sales. We trust a company in business ten years more than one just begun.

Initially, new posts can be easy to rank well in search engines. This is because they are in an evaluation stage. Over time, the performance of the page will determine its true long term relevant position. Search engines know what appears in their search results and they know which posts were clicked on by users (indicating user interest). If a post does not receive clicks, it tends to eventually fall further down the ranking results. We should assume Zazzle marketplace rankings follow similar concepts. Quality designs receiving clicks and sales should rise to the top.

Each of your products is essentially a post on the Zazzle website, so as you read more about optimization, always be asking yourself if this new tactic can be applied in some way to your store.

Price & Sales

One way price impacts ranking is similar to what we've already discussed. If your item is the most expensive in the search results, your item will most likely receive less clicks, and over time, this "lack of customer interest" could slowly slip you lower in the marketplace results.

Sales are another indicator of user interest. When something is selling, it's logical that Zazzle will want to display it higher in the marketplace results. All your efforts to increase sales should also help you rank higher.

Traffic

Without traffic, no one can buy your item. When you think about optimization, keep these possible traffic sources in mind:

- Zazzle Marketplace
- Social Media Network Links
- Referrals from Associates,
- Blogs
- Forums (not just Zazzle)
- Email Marketing and/or Newsletters
- Search Engines
- Video Marketing
- Advertising

Image Tips

After you know your keywords and know there's a demand for your product, start thinking about images. Here are some tips:

- You can create your own images, purchase royalty free commercial use photos, or use public domain images.

- Accept that you cannot protect your images 100% when selling on the Internet. Before you chase down someone who has *stolen* your image, consider that your time might be better spent creating and promoting.

- To create the copyright symbol ©: hold down your ALT key and type +0169

- Even if you "Lock" your images (discussed later) or place text with your store name on your item, when you allow customization, a determined buyer can simply cover your image or text with their own image.

- Use the bulk uploader if you have a lot of images.

- Create your images as large as possible and let Zazzle scale them down for smaller products. Abstracts might be designed at 6000 x 6000 pixels.

- If you're using photography, you might use the default pixels of your camera when creating designs. (We use our SLR camera's highest resolution of 4752 x 3168 pixels.)

- It may help with SEO to rename your images with keywords prior to uploading. Instead of using _MG_245.jpg for your file name, use: long-stemmed-red-rose.jpg.

- Category thumbnails images are 324 × 324 pixels. Zazzle will scale larger images down, leaving white space around them if needed to make the image square.

- Use your software: Try filters or effects like water drops, distress, textures, feather edges, or black and white.

Custom Templates and Quick Create

At this point, you know your target audience, you've researched your keywords, and you have a plan as to how your design will be found by a buyer. It's time to begin creating products.

Creating a single product is not difficult to figure out on your own, so we'll advance forward to creating a template.

A template is a place holder for either text or an image. There are two reasons sellers create templates:

1. *Customer Personalization:* The template holds a place for the buyer to customize. Think of things like business cards, wedding invitations, or luggage tags that require the user to input information (a name, address, or date).

2. *Quick Create:* The template holds a place for the seller to add an image. This is used for batch processing, where one image is quickly applied to numerous products at once.

Understanding Templates

First, let's illustrate what templates do. Two postcards are shown below. The phrase "Your Text Here" implies that the user should change the text. Both these products use templates.

In the first postcard image, the customer must click *Customize* to change the text or image.

In the second postcard image, the template fields are immediately visible, so the customer can easily change the text or image, without clicking "Customize."

Template where the buyer must click *Customize It!* to change text

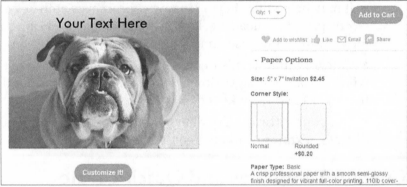

Template where the customer can personalize immediately

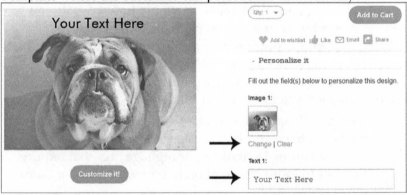

The second item was created using a setting called *Allow Editing on Product Page*. This is the preferable setting when you want the customer to easily add customization. (We will show you how to use this setting later.)

Another Template Example:

This note card contains three *immediately visible* template fields: two images and the text field containing the word "Child." The rest of the design is initially hidden. You want to present a simple *call to action*. Most buyers will only want to add their child's name and make the purchase. Customers don't need to be distracted by seeing the rest of the design.

In this example (the card above), it is still possible for the buyer to change the main text. If the buyer clicks "Customize it!" (shown above), all text fields are revealed (as shown below):

Buyer's view of the same card after clicking "Customize it!"

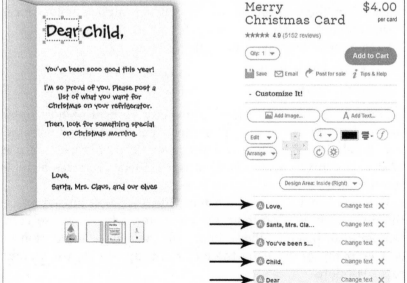

Create Your Template Folders

The first step to creating templates is to create the folders that will contain them. Go to *Products* > *All Categories* > *Add New Category*. You will see the image below. Note that there is an option to keep the category *hidden*. Be careful here and make sure you check this box. You want your templates hidden and not posted live to the Zazzle marketplace.

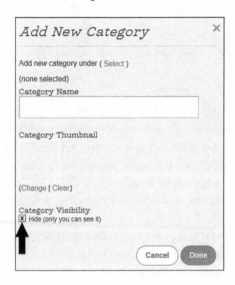

We will help you create some templates to be used for Quick Create. You'll create one set of templates as a place holder for a horizontal image, and another set, for a vertical image.

Create the following hidden category folders:

- My Horizontal
- My Vertical

For setting this up, choose to use any vertical or horizontal image that you like. It doesn't matter what the image illustrates. It will help if the image is a size you will typically use. We use 4752 × 3168 pixels which is what our camera produces at high resolution.

When we make the hidden templates, we will always place the image centered on the products. Later, when you use your templates to produce *Public* items, you will have the option to edit your image by using the left, right, up, down, rotate, and re-size options.

96 Products in a Category Folder

As you begin to create your product templates, consider how you will keep your Quick Create folders organized. We've made one horizontal and one vertical folder (category) so far.

Quick Create allows you to create up to 100 products at a time, but Zazzle's editor only allows you to select up to 96 items in a folder at once.

You can change the title, description, category, tags, additional information, and royalty for all 96 items with only a few clicks.

With this in mind, you might limit each Quick Create folder to 96 items. This way you can post them to a new folder and easily make bulk edits.

If you happen to have 192 items in a folder, you can sort them and bulk edit, by choosing 96 items at a time. The main thing to remember is to never let a Quick Create folder go above 100 items, or some products will not be created during batch processing.

Create a Template

To create a pocket journal template, select: *Create > Office Products > See All Office Products > Notebooks & Journals > Pocket Journals* and click the image to open up the product creation screen.

• Click *Select Image* and add your horizontal image.

• Rotate/re-size your image to fit nicely as a horizontal cover.

• Add the same image again, and re-size/rotate it to use as a back cover similar to our dog in the image below.

• Click *Add Text*. Enter your Zazzle store URL in this format: http://Zazzle.com/StoreName*/ (change *StoreName* to your store name) and re-size this text to fit on the back cover. If needed, use decimals (i.e.: 1.4) to set the font size. Leave the font color set to black since it can always be changed during the Quick Create process.

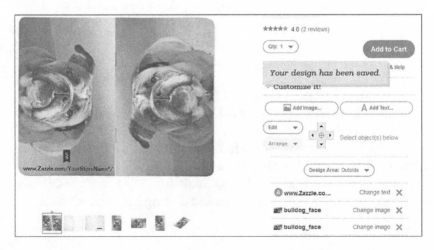

Set the Template Feature:

• Click the little gear icon (see the first arrow below) to open the *Advanced Options* pop-up drop-down menu

• You will see some options here that we will not be using in this example, but you should be aware they exist.

— *Tile this image:* Repeats the image multiple times on the product

— *Show whites in image as transparent:* Allows color to show through any white areas giving a stencil effect

— *Lock object(s):* Freezes image or text. Buyers can't edit it, but they can place an image over whatever is locked.

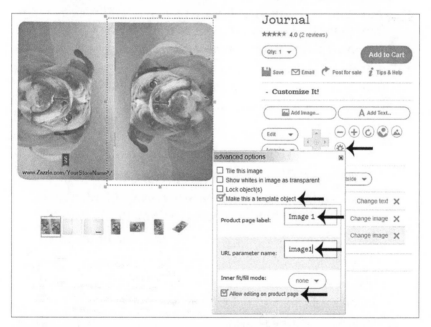

• *Make this a template object:* Check this box.

• *Product page label:* Change the 0 to a 1 being careful to leave the spacing, so it reads: Image 1. (The *Label* provides guidance for the customer. Text labels might use *Name, Address 1,* etc.)

• *URL parameter name:* Change this to Image1 being careful not to use space between characters. For Quick Create to work, the parameters must match on all items. The system will replace all Image1 objects with your uploaded image. (For text, use Text1)

— Never use trademark names in parameters. Use a label like "Registered at store #1" but never a real store name.

• *Allow editing on product page:* Check this box. As we explained earlier, this allows your customer to have the option to change the template field immediately (in this case, your image) without having to click *Customize.*

> * *Note*: As a reminder, if you were creating a complex design, you might choose NOT to check *Allow Editing on Product Page* on certain elements. This would hide the elements from a customer's view. (The earlier Santa card example would have left this unchecked for the main interior text.)

• Close the *Advanced options* box.

• Repeat these steps to place the same image on the back cover. Use the same parameters of Image 1 for *Label* and Image1 for *Parameter Name*. Do not change these to Image 2. By keeping the same parameter name, Quick Create will add your new image in both locations. Also, if a buyer uploads their own image, it will appear immediately on both the front and back cover.

• *Lock Your URL:* Select your text by clicking the URL text. Click the gear again and place a check in the *Lock Objects* box.

• Click *Post For Sale* and complete the content information
  — *Title:* My Horizontal
  — *Description:* My Horizontal
  — *Category:* Art (You have to choose something here)
  — *Events* and *Occasions* and *Recipient:* leave blank (Since the item will be hidden, these won't matter.)
  — *Store Category:* My Horizontal (This is one of the folders you created earlier.)
  — *Tags:* Horizontal
  — *Suitable Audience:* Rated G
  — *Product Visibility:* Hidden
  — *Make product a template:* Yes
  — *Show "Customize it" button:* Yes
  — *Royalty:* Enter your royalty. (Remember to nudge your royalty percentage as high as possible, while keeping your desired sale price.)

• *User Agreement:* Place a check mark and click *Post It*

The confirmation page should show you a link to your *Hidden* item.

Create Zazzle Default Templates

Next, we'll use Zazzle's default *Quick create* to quickly add additional horizontal templates. This process may take you a *few hours* to complete and must be done in *one sitting*. You cannot exit out and return later. Go to *My Products > Quick create.*

Under *Choose products to create*, choose *Use Zazzle defaults*, and select *All Products.*

Next, click *Your Image Here* and add your horizontal image.

Leave *Choose fit/fill option* set at *Use template defaults.*

Click *Done,* and your horizontal image will display on the items set in Zazzle's default list, just like the image below, but each item will have your own horizontal image on it.

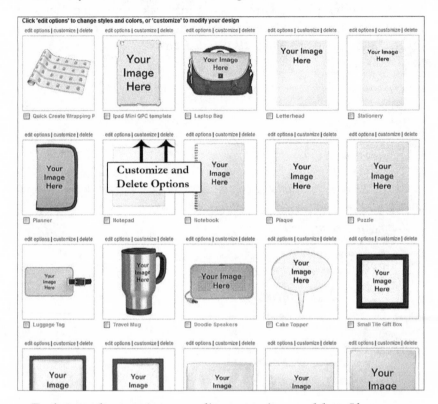

Each item has options to *edit, customize,* or *delete.* If you see a caution on any item, indicated by an exclamation point — delete that item. This happens when the image is too small for the item.

Next, you're going to customize EACH item. Go to your first item and click *customize.* Leave your image centered, but re-size it if necessary, so it looks nice on the product.

Next you have to change the parameters and make sure *Allow editing on product page* is checked. Click the gear icon, as you learned earlier. In general, you will change the product label from *Cover Image* to *Image 1* with a space, and change the parameter name from *CoverImage* to *Image1* with no space.

If there is an item that you wish to always include text for the customer, such as "Your Text Here." Add that text box now, and using the gear icon, change the parameters to *Text 1* and *Text1.* On some items such as a luggage tag, you might add more specific guidance in the page label parameter for the customer. You might use something like this for Product page label/URL parameter name respectively: Your Name/Text1, Phone/Text2, Address/Text3, and Zip Code/Text4.

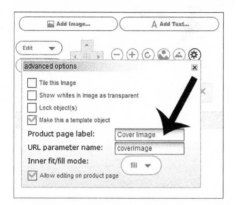

Two Images: If there is an item that you wish always to have two identical images, such as we did on the pocket journal earlier, add this second image now. Add your same horizontal image and use the gear option to change the parameters for this second image to *Image 1* and *Image1*. When the item looks acceptable, close the pop-up window and move on to the next item.

Repeat this for all 98 items. You want them all to have the same parameters and your horizontal image to be centered, but sized properly. You are making the page labels and parameters match what we used earlier on your journal.

When Zazzle releases new products, you will continue to use *Image1* in your templates.

After your edits are complete for all 98 items, click *Next.* This will bring you to the *Post For Sale* area. Complete it as follows:

- *Title:* My Horizontal
- *Description:* My Horizontal
- *Category:* Art
- *Events* and *Occasions* and *Recipient:* leave blank (Because the item will be hidden, these don't matter)
- *Store Category:* My Horizontal
- *Tags:* Horizontal

The next part has your *Additional Information,* and you will notice that the Quick Create *Post for Sale* screen is slightly different from the single product *Post for Sale* screen.

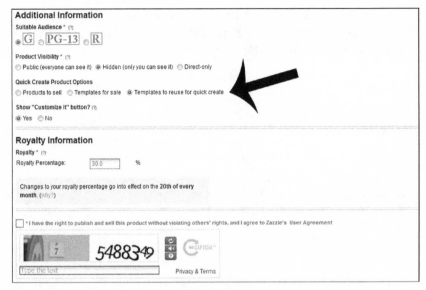

- *Suitable Audience*: Choose *Rated G*

- *Product Visibility*: Choose *Hidden* (we are adding this group of items to your hidden horizontal category folder)

- *Quick Create Product Options*: This relates to how your products will be used. Choose: *Templates to reuse for quick create.* Here's some guidance on these options:

  * *Products to sell:* Creates No template fields (best used when you don't expect the customer to edit anything)

  * *Templates for sale:* Creates template products with text or images which customers can customize before purchasing. When used with *"Allow edit on Product Page,"* a customer can edit without clicking customize.

  * *Templates to reuse for quick create:* Creates templates you will use to create new products in bulk. All images and text will be templates and can be used for batch creation, assuming their parameters match.

- *Royalty*: Enter a royalty for your quick create products. This will apply to all the products, but after they are created, you can edit them individually if you like.

- *User Agreement:* place a check mark, complete the captcha, and click *Post It.* Quick Create items will take about 24 hours to appear in the hidden category in your store.

Repeat this procedure again, but use your vertical image and *My Vertical* for the title, description, tags, and store category folder.

Check Your Royalties

When you created Zazzle's default templates, you entered a royalty for all 98 items. This was an efficient use of your time, but recall that you can nudge royalty percentages to increase your take-home pay without raising the customer's price. Before using Quick Create templates to create *Public* items, review your rates for *each* individual product. Under *Account > Products*, choose use the Action drop-down option, select *Edit > Royalty Rate*, and adjust the rate for each template to maximize your profits.

Pricing

In addition to these small increases in price, you might consider setting significantly higher royalty for certain product types. For example, posters can often be set at a 65% royalty and still appear to be a reasonable price to a buyer.

Visit the marketplace and check the price of similar top ranking products. Since sales impact rankings, initially, you might set a price lower than these products. If you beat your competition on price and this generates views and sales, you should eventually be competitive for their positions. Once you've reached page one for your keywords, you can begin to nudge up your royalties and hopefully, maintain your position and sales.

You also have a default royalty setting found at *Account > Seller Account > Default Royalty*. Here you can set a royalty to apply to every new product you create or set it to apply to both your newly created (future products) and existing products.

Using Quick Create Templates

When your Quick Create templates appear inside your hidden horizontal and vertical folders, you can use them for *Public* items.

Go to: *Products > Quick Create,* but this time don't choose the Zazzle default, and instead, look for *Use Your Own Templates,* and click *Select.* Choose My Horizontal folder (assuming you will be using a horizontal image) and you will see your default image, the one you used to make your templates, automatically appear inside the image box.

Click *Change.* Upload your new image to use for *Public* products. Leave the defaults for Choose Fit/Fill Options and click *Done.*

The next page should show your image on all your templates. Use the customize option to edit any images that do not look nice. Work your way down the page editing each item as needed and deleting anything with a caution. Then, click *Next.*

Completely fill out the *Post for Sale* page, but this time, **do NOT click Hidden**, and instead, click *Public (everyone can see it).* Also make sure the *Show "Customize it"* option says "Yes," and that you have chosen the correct *Quick Create Product Options.* When in doubt, always choose *Templates to reuse for Quick Create.*

If you changed some of your royalties as we suggested, your royalty field will have a message: "Your selected products have different royalties set (change this)." Just leave this alone because you know your royalties are set to maximize your income.

When you finish all the entries, click *Post it.*

Quick Create Issues

There are two common issues when using Quick Create. The first is you notice that some products do not show your new image. They show the horizontal image you used for templates. This happens when you've missed a consistent parameter. To solve this, cancel this entire batch. Open the flawed template, fix the parameter, and re-post for sale. Go back into your hidden folder and delete the flawed item. Since you fixed a single product, the fixed item should have published immediately, so you can try your Quick Create process again. You don't have to wait 24 hours.

The second issue is Quick Create locks up and you can't click *customize.* If you have already edited over half the group, write down the last product you correctly edited on a piece of paper. Try to delete every product including and after the item that froze. (If you can't do this, you'll have to cancel the entire batch.) Click *Next* to publish all products that were edited correctly.

Go back into Quick Create and process again using the same image. When you see all the products, delete every product up to the point you noted on your paper (because you already published these items). Then use the customize option to edit the remaining (which are new products) and continue to publish normally.

Grouping

Zazzle uses a grouping system for similar items. This means that if you create 200 items, it may appear as if your store has a much smaller inventory. For example, ornaments might be grouped and count as one item. You can find a detailed sticky post explanation at: *Zazzle Forum > Zazzle Public Forums > Your Zazzle Store*:

http://forum.zazzle.com/gallery/a_graphical_guide_to_grouping_aka_where_are_my

New Product Announcements

Sometimes Zazzle announces new products on a weekly basis. You'll need to have a system to keep track of which images you've used and on what items. We suggest you create templates for all new releases and place them together in a new hidden folder. After you've accumulated a significant group, you can run all your images through this folder using Quick Create.

Alternatively, you can create the new product as a template and when you publish for sale, click the link that says "Go there now."

Customize this new template by adding your next image. Keep repeating this process for all images. Using this link retains some entry fields and eliminates some clicks to help you create faster.

Associates: Affiliate Marketing

As mentioned, Zazzle associates (also referred to as affiliates) earn income by referring people to Zazzle. You can receive a 15% referral commission when a user clicks through your link and makes a purchase of *any item* on Zazzle. These referral sales help you achieve your Volume Sales Bonus.

We've discussed the logic behind immediately using the Associate program as part of your business plan. It's simply another potential source of income for you to have while you're busy designing your own products.

This chapter highlights numerous strategies to increase your referrals for the best Return on Investment, the best use of your time — for the income received.

Confusion with Referrals

Referrals are cookie based. This means a "cookie" must be set on the user's hard drive prior to completing a purchase in order for you, the associate, to earn your referral commission. Computer cookies last 45 days. The sad fact is, sometimes, the cookie does not get set even if you provide a proper referral link. Here are some examples why you might not receive a referral commission:

• The user has set their computer to block cookies.

• The user clicks through your link, but for whatever reason does not complete the purchase at that time. Later, the user makes the purchase — but from a different computer.

• The user clicks through your link, but at some time between the click and the actual purchase, the user clears their browser's cache (which clears the cookie).

• The user clicks on your link, but there is a blocker in place. Zazzle protects the first cookie set for 11 hours. If the user has visited Zazzle before clicking your link, perhaps through someone else's referral link or search engine results, there is a blocker that prevents your new cookie from registering. Your new referral cookie will not override this *original one*. This generally protects the original referral and ensures the first cookie set will receive the commission for the sale. This 11 hour cookie is a *session* or *browser* cookie.

Publicize Your Store's Referral URL

An easy way to earn referrals is to publicize your store URL with your referral code attached. You can publicize your store with an * (also referred to as the *Zazzle star*) or share your store with your referral ID coded as in:

- http://Zazzle.com/StoreName*/
- http://Zazzle.com/StoreName?rf=000000000000000000/

Replace *StoreName* with the name of your store and always end your URL with a front slash, as shown above. Replace the zeros with your own Associate ID number. It's best to use the full Associate ID format because some sites will strip the * out of the first URL shown above.

When you are signed into Zazzle, you'll find your referral (associate) ID at:

http://Zazzle.com/my/associate/associate/

Often you will just share the URL to promote your store, but there will be times when you want to create a link using HTML coding. To code a simple link to your store, you would write:

<a href="http://zazzle.com/StoreName?rf=000000000000000000/">
StoreName</a>

To code a link to your store from a blog you own use:

<a href="http://zazzle.com/StoreName?rf=000000000000000000/"
rel="nofollow">StoreName</a>

The additional code of rel="nofollow" tells Google not to send any *link juice* (not to give any SEO weight or relevancy points to the site you are linking to—in this case, Zazzle). Google has suggested we include this in all of our associate links.

This practice was established because many businesses were abusing links. They would purchase numerous links to a site as a strategy, to make the site seem more *relevant* than others. To control these *paid links*, Google expects site owners to add rel="nofollow" to any link that can potentially earn you money, whether you were paid to place it on your site, or you're placing it there to earn future income.

Tracking Codes

A tracking code is something you add to your referral URL so that when you view your reports, you can trace where the sale actually came from. To add a tracking code, place &tc=code to the end of a referral URL. (Change *code* to something that will indicate where you are placing this link.)

http://Zazzle.com/StoreName?rf=000000000000000000&tc=code/

You can use upper and lower case letters in your tracking code to make it easier to read when it appears in your item description of your Referral Report. The image below shows a tracking code of LABlog.

Here are some places where you might use tracking codes:

• *Social Media:* Codes to designate Facebook, Twitter, YouTube, Google+, and so forth.

• *Blog Posts:* Codes for your blog, maybe even segregated further to specific categories in your blog.

• *Email:* Code to track sales from an email campaign

• *Business Cards:* Include a tracking code on your store URL. Consider using a URL shortener (discussed later) to save space. You might also create special business cards with a unique code to track sales from a specific conference you attend.

• *Printed Media:* Use tracking codes on anything you print, such as a flyer or an ad in you local newspaper.

Go back to each of the social sites you set up earlier, and find where you listed your store URL. Change this URL to the format used above—add your Associate ID (instead of using the Zazzle star) and add a unique tracking code for each site. You can also make this change in the redirect that you set up for your domain name. Add a code to begin tracking visitors who might type in your domain name directly into their browser.

Share from Zazzle

The easiest way to begin marketing for referral income is to use the built in Zazzle *Share* option. When you are logged in on Zazzle and see a product you like, click the *Share* option. When the drop-down menu opens, choose the social network you wish to post to.

Sometimes, there is an option to add your own comments to personalize your shared post. This is a good place for you to add your keywords with hashtags and use language to encourage the viewer to click through.

Sometimes, you have the option to edit the URL, which is great because you can add your tracking code to it—before you send. Below, we've added a tracking code to a Twitter share:

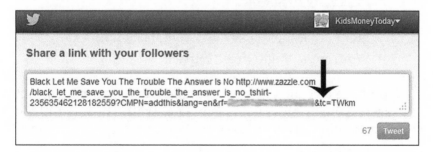

Interaction with Google Analytics

Google Analytics only tracks your store pages, so it will not track any product page shares. Because of this, you might want to also manually post your storefront, category, and department URLs to social media networks. Start this as soon as you've created items so you'll have some results show up in your analytic reports (which we will discuss later).

URL Shorteners

A URL shortener takes a very long URL and creates a shorter URL in it's place. This is also referred to as a redirect. The new shorter URL will redirect the user to the long URL.

Some reasons to use a URL shortener are:

- It simply looks nicer to the viewer.
- It is another method of tracking clicks. Many shorteners have reports showing how often they've been clicked, and these reports give you valuable information to make better marketing decisions.
- It creates a short URL for your store that you can place on products, business cards, and other advertising.
- It can be used for list building (shorten an opt-in URL).

Some examples of URL shortener services are:

- http://bitly.com/
- http://goo.gl/
- http://tinyURL.com/
- Wordpress Plugin (paid) http://KidsandMoneyToday.com/track-link
- Wordpress plugin (free): Jetpack

If you have a created a short URL and want to check where it goes and ensure that it's pulling in your Associate ID and tracking code, you might use one of these free services:

- http://expandURL.appspot.com/
- http://longURL.org/expand

Simply copy in a short URL and these services will show you all the redirect paths lying beneath the shortened URL. When you are checking your own shortened links, you should see your Associate ID and tracking code listed.

Create Landing Pages

Category Pages

A landing page is the page a customer "lands" on after clicking your promotional link. We've previously discussed links to your store and using unique tags to group items for description links. Another way to create a landing page consisting of a group of items is to link to a category page. When you are viewing a category page, copy the URL in your browser. It will be in this format:

http://zazzle.com/StoreName/gifts?cg=000000000000000000

Next, add the parameters for your tracking code and Associate ID to ensure you receive your 15% referral commission:

http://zazzle.com/StoreName/gifts?cg=000000000000000000 &tc=CODE&rf=000000000000000000

There are no spaces in the URL above. You could use this URL in a promotional link to show off groups of items, and if it's your own category, you'll earn both royalties and referrals on any sales.

Wishlists

If you want to pick and choose products from different stores to promote, you can create a *customized landing page* by using Wishlists. They allow you to group items and display them under a single URL. The Wishlist setting is found in your account, as an option under *My Account at a Glance*:

My Account at a glance

- My Profile
- Order History
- Account Settings
- Notifications
- Default Royalty
- Wishlist ◀——
- Review your purchase

Select *Wishlist* and click *Add New* to open the option to create a Name and Description for your list. Under *Other options*, check *Set as Default list* so the items you select will automatically be added into this list.

These lists can be set to *Private* or *Public*, which means they're also searchable. You might use this description box to create a very customized SEO friendly page that could be indexed by Google. You might choose Private if you did freelance work and were creating custom items for a company event, a family reunion, or a school club—anywhere that you would not want the public to view the items.

To add items to a Wishlist, when you are on the product page, look near the Share button and click the heart icon *Add to wishlist*:

The product will automatically be added to the list you currently have set as *Default*. As you create multiple lists, and want to add more items to a particular list, you will need to remember to first go into your Wishlist settings and make sure your desired list is set as the *Default* list.

You'll probably have many ideas for Wishlists. You could create a set of matching monogrammed items to "Purchase for the bride" or have a Halloween list to share in October. You could create a list by product type (such as mugs). You might browse Pinterest boards for more ideas on how to group topics.

When you click Wishlist inside the back-end of your store, the opening screen is similar to your category screen. All your Wishlists appear in the left menu. The center of the page contains options such as *Edit, Delete,* and *View This List,* which shows you the customer view. There is a little box below each product, along with an action arrow to open a drop-down list to reorder your items, but one thing you cannot do is move an item from one list to another.

Seller view of WishLists:

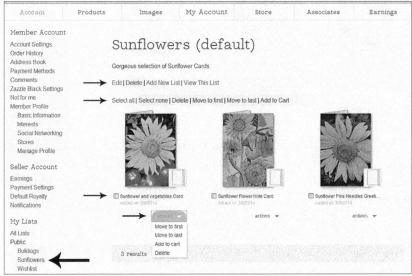

Your Wishlist (Landing Page) URL: Find your Wishlist ID by looking in your browser when you have your wishlist selected. To create a link to your wishlist page, use the format below, but change *WishlistID* to your ID number, replace the zeros with your Associate ID number, and add your own tracking code.

http://zazzle.com/pd/list?wl=**WishlistID**&rf=000000000000000000 &tc=**code**

The Wishlist URL for the sunflower cards (with no a referral or tracking code) is:

http://Zazzle.com/pd/list?wl=119607407397670833

The image below shows the layout the buyer will see when they click your promotional Wishlist link. It includes your title, a link to your profile, and your description (which could be much longer than what we entered for this example).

Buyer view of WishLists:

Collections

Zazzle describes Collections as curated custom landing pages. You create one URL containing items of your choice with a related theme. Similar to Wishlists, you can then take this URL and use it for promotion.

To create a Collection, use the following URL format:

http://zazzle.com/pd/collection?rf=00000000000000000&lst=PID, PID,PID&tc=code

Note that it contains your Associate ID, tracking code and Product Identification numbers (PIDs) for each of your desired items. You separate PIDs with commas (in this case, it is three items).

The URL has no spaces. Make sure you are using &lst which uses a lower case l as in list, not the number one (as in &1st). You also need to use an authentic referral URL or the coding fails and redirects to Zazzle's home page.

To find the Product ID for the item you wish to add, you can look at the URL in your browser while on the product page and copy the number at the very end. Alternatively, you can scroll down the product page and see the ID listed under *Other Info*.

Here's an example URL for a Collection containing the same three items that we previously used in the Wishlist discussion:

http://zazzle.com/pd/collection?rf=000000000000000000&lst=1374 10202140924635,137556603380933421,137581274578858295&tc=code

If you replace the zeros with an authentic Associate ID, your browser will display the image below:

Buyer view of Collections:

Collections are not perfect. When the URL is loaded in a browser, the commas change to %2c, so you can't copy the browser URL to a new location. Also, if the user were to refresh the browser, the effect is the same as re-loading the URL containing %2c. You lose all the items and instead, the Zazzle home page will display.

WishList vs. Collection

Both methods are time consuming. Collections display a left menu of other options, so they might easily convert curious customers.

Our preference is Wishlists, where you can create a custom title and description, plus a link to your profile. Also, when the user scrolls over items, a pop-up shows two additional links: *Designed by YourStore* and *See on # Styles or # Products*. The Wishlist layout is also more like a "Squeeze Page," which means the viewers' choices are limited. The only choices are to click the items you have presented. You've forced them down a funnel which will hopefully result in a sale.

Promote with RSS Feeds

RSS stands for Rich Site Summary (also referred to as Really Simple Syndication). In simple terms, this is a line of coding that pulls and displays information from a designated source. In our case, it will pull products from Zazzle. You will add your referral code to it and share this feed to market information across the Internet. This brings traffic to Zazzle and you get paid for these qualifying referral sales.

Referral feeds can include metadata information such as full or summarized text from descriptions, publishing dates, title, image, and authorship (the store name). Here are some ideas for how you might pull feeds from Zazzle:

- *Store name:* Pull all products from a specific store
- *Product types:* Pull only mugs
- *Theme:* Pull only "Cat" items
- *Quantity:* Pull only 3 items
- *Creation Date:* Pull only "New" items
- *Popularity:* Pull popular items based on Zazzle's secret algorithm (a mixture of views, sales, comments, clicks, etc.)

These attributes can be combined. For example, you could pull all new St. Patrick's Day cards from a specific store.

Note: We will be discussing both free and fee based methods of RSS promotion. We suggest you learn both and practice a mixture of both in your marketing efforts. They are all based on software and by using a mixture of both, you will always have something promoting even if one platform fails to perform.

Google Base and RSS Feeds

There are two formats for feeds:

- *Standard RSS format* looks like this:
  http://feed.zazzle.com/StoreName/**rss?**{parameters}
- *Other feeds* look like this:
  http://feed.zazzle.com/StoreName/**feed?**{parameters}
- A *Google Base feed* looks like this
  http://feed.zazzle.com/StoreName/**feed?ft=gb**{parameters}

In this book, we will focus on using the Standard RSS format. We will discuss what makes up a feed, provide some examples, and then suggest how you might use these feeds in your marketing.

Create Your Store's Referral RSS Feed

To create your store feed, use this structure, but change *StoreName* to your store:

http://feed.zazzle.com/StoreName/rss/

To add your associate referral code using *Standard RSS format*, we add the ?at parameter attribute with your Associate ID like this:

http://feed.zazzle.com/StoreName/rss?at=000000000000000000/

Note the difference from the structure of a store referral URL:

http://zazzle.com/StoreName?rf=000000000000000000/

You will use *?at* instead of *?rf* in the URL. You can type both URLs into Firefox to see how an RSS feed results in a list of items and the store URL takes your visitor to your store's home page.

Three Most Common RSS Feed Errors

1. *Type of Feed:* Mixing up the coding structure between the rules for the RSS store feed and those for Google Base.

2. *Referral Coding Parameter:* Mixing up the *rf* and *at* in coding.

3. *Coding with & instead of ?*: The first parameter in a feed is always preceded by ? and all other parameters will be preceded by the & sign. The order of parameters may be changed around — as long as the **first parameter is always preceded by the question mark.** For example, these two feeds below use *at* for the Associate ID and FB for the tracking code, and they will produce the same results.

feed.zazzle.com/StoreName/rss?at=000000000000000000&tc=FB
feed.zazzle.com/StoreName/rss?tc=FB&at=000000000000000000

The important thing is the ? always comes prior to the first parameter and it is *used only once in a feed.* Thereafter, you always use the & sign when adding any parameter.

Sample Feeds

Pull a Certain Number of Products

There will be times when you only want to show a distinct number of products. For example, when you post to social media, you don't want to send 96 associate products to your followers. That would be very spammy.

To limit the number of products displayed, we must add an additional parameter to the coding. The parameter *ps* refers to *Page Size* or number of products per page.

Add it to the end of your feed using &ps= with a number that will represent how many products you want to appear in the feed.

For example, to show only one item in a feed use this format:

feed.zazzle.com/StoreName/rss?at=000000000000000000&ps=1

To limit your feed to three products use:

feed.zazzle.com/StoreName/rss?at=000000000000000000&ps=3

Popularity and New Item Feeds

Use the parameter st for *Sort Type* to pull your popular or new items (date_created).

For a feed of your most popular items (based on Zazzle's secret popularity algorithm) use:

feed.zazzle.com/StoreName/rss?at=000000000000000000&st=popularity

You can use new or date_created for recent items. This will pull a feed of the latest items you created:

feed.zazzle.com/StoreName/rss?at=000000000000000000&st=new

Unique Theme or Product Line Feeds

Use the *Query String* parameter *qs* to stream products with a common theme or unique niche. It can be a product line like *mug* or a keyword such as *cat*.

This would pull items from a store that contain the tag *cat*:

feed.zazzle.com/StoreName/rss?at=000000000000000000&qs=cat

You can pull from the *entire marketplace* by omitting your store name. This feed pulls 3 cat mugs from the entire marketplace.

feed.zazzle.com/rss?at=000000000000000000&ps=3&qs=cat+mug

If you added a special tag to items within your store, you could use this tag to pull a unique feed. For example, if you added *mysold* as a Power Tag to your sold items, you could pull a feed for only your *items sold*.

feed.zazzle.com/StoreName/rss?at=000000000000000000&qs=mysold

This unique tag has to be in the first ten tags of the item, your *Power Tags*. To go in and add these tags takes time, so you might evaluate whether the Return on Investment is worth it. Would your time be better spent doing other things for your business?

Tracking Parameter

We discussed the *Tracking* parameter when creating referral URLs and sharing to social media. You can use the same parameter, *tc* in RSS feeds. Follow the same coding rules. Add the parameter with the & sign.

The feed below will pull from a store with our referral ID, a page sized for 3 items, with a query string of *cat*, a sort type of newly created, and sales will be tracked with the code *Blog*:

feed.zazzle.com/StoreName/rss?at=000000000000000000&ps=3
&qs=cat&st=new&tc=Blog

RSS Feed Parameters

Here's a list of parameters from the Zazzle RSS Guide:

- **at** *Associate Referral ID*: Adds your referral code
- **bg** *Background color*: a string in the form RRGGBB
- **cg** *Category*: Zazzle gallery product line.
- **ft** *Feed type*: Value can be either "rss" for RSS or "gb" for Google Base. If not specified, defaults to RSS.
- ~~**gl** gl=StoreName used to display the custom store skin as opposed to displaying in the marketplace~~. Custom store colors was discontinued in 2013, so this is just provided for your information (in case you see it discussed anywhere, and wonder what it is).
- **isz** *Image size*: The size of the product images in your feed. Set to "tiny"for 50 pixels, "small" 92 pixels, "medium" 152 pixels, "large" 210 pixels, "huge" 328 pixels, or specify the exact number as: &isz=300
- **pg** *Page number:* Specifies the result page on which the feed starts.
  - Tip: You can add ?pg=15 to the end of any Zazzle URL and this will jump you forward to page 15. When browsing Zazzle, you can use this to skip pages to discover unique items not yet ranking well in the marketplace.
- **ps** *Page size*: The number of products per page.
- **qs** *Query string:* Use to pull products by text fields, unique keywords, and product types.
- **st** *Sort type:* Value can be "popularity," "date_created." or "new"
- ~~**sp** Sort period, used for a time frame and popularity sorts. Value can be: 0=store history, 1=today, 7=this week, 30=this month.~~ *Sort period* has not functioned properly, but is provided for your information (in case it should start working again, you see it discussed anywhere, or you wonder what it is,).

- **tc** *Tracking code*: Use this to trace where your sales clicks originated

- **vm** *View:* &vm=list will force a list view (as opposed to grid view).

- ~~**pt** *Product type*~~, hasn't been working, see notes below and instead use cg or qs parameters

The following forum excerpt explains more on the *pt* parameter:

"Yes the RSS documentation still references the pt parameter. Technically it does still work, but grouped products get un-grouped when using it, which is what everyone using pt= complains about. If you use the department name in the query string, it works fine.

Generally, using whatever is after the underscore in the product type will work, but sometimes it will be too generic. i.e. skinit_case, If you use Case, you are going to get all sorts of different cases and may not be the specific one you want. The best way to find the specific one right now would be to go to [Zazzle] and start selecting the department that you want and you will get to many lower level departments. Electronics > Cases > iphone+5+cases > etc.

There is nothing technical about the switch. It was done for easier usability.

1. You don't need to know the specific pt name

2. You can get multiple brands in one feed using departments over one product type with pt

3. Whatever product you want, if you add that name to the query string, it will most likely work because there are many variations for each department (gift-box, trinket+box, jewelry+box, etc)." Source:
http://forum.zazzle.com/tools/broken_rss_feed_mechanism

When creating RSS feeds, you might find a product list useful:
http://Zazzle.com/sell/affiliates/promotionaltools/rss

Also find the RSS Guide here:
http://asset.zcache.com/assets/graphics/z2/mk/sell/RSSGuide1.03.pdf

Auto-posting Products

You can save time by finding ways to automate your referral posts. Instead of spending time manually sharing links, you can be designing items or researching new unique target audiences.

Most auto-posting is set up to post information to social networks like Facebook and Twitter, but it is also possible to auto-post to a blog.

Auto-posting gives the appearance of activity on a site. Not too many people will follow someone who only posts once a month, or worse, once a quarter. Social networks are constantly updating their algorithms and they tend to reward the active people who are regularly posting and interacting on the site. Inactive pages without fresh material don't get shown very well.

One common question social media marketers have is whether they should post the same information on each social network. There's a concern that we should not post the same item to Facebook, Twitter, Google+, and so on.

The average Internet user tends to have a favorite social media site. They are usually *not active* everywhere, not following the same person or business on every network. This makes it fairly safe to say that it is perfectly acceptable to have some posts auto-post everywhere. The majority of our followers will not see the duplication, and those who do, will most likely be forgiving.

We, as social media marketers, do need to be everywhere. In between our auto-posting, we will add the occasional human factors: respond to a comment, like someone's comment, share a post from others, and so forth.

When you're auto-posting Zazzle products, your goal should be to create a referral post with: a title, an image, no price, and a tracking link back to Zazzle. It is also beneficial if you are able to include a hashtag symbol with a keyword so you can group your social post to others within a network.

As we've mentioned, don't place all your efforts into one type of auto-posting. This way if one fails, others will continue and this lessens any decrease in your income. Social media auto-posting is notoriously finicky. Every time a social network changes something, every platform responsible for creating the auto-posts needs to adjust. Some issues might take a few weeks to sort out or might not be supported for a year or more, and then could come back. Working this type of marketing requires a lot of patience.

IFTTT

One free method of auto-posting is *IFTTT (If This, Then That)*:
http://ifttt.com/

The site is very user friendly. It helps you create recipe actions that say, "If this occurs," please "Do that."

After you create your account, you will take a customized RSS Feed (using the information we taught earlier) and place it in the "This" section. You're setting a trigger that tells IFTTT, "If you find a new item in *this* Zazzle RSS Feed" then, do *that*. The *that* entry can be: "Post to Facebook, " "Post to Twitter," "Post to a Blog," or even "Send an email."

IFTTT connects with many different platforms. One advantage of IFTTT is it has the capability to post to both a Facebook Profile and Facebook Page. However, at the time of this writing, IFTTT does not include posting to Google+ Pages or Profiles.

The instructions or commands used on the site are referred to as a *Recipe*. You can create as many recipes as you like, and you can explore recipes created and shared by other people.

IFTTT does not retain your tracking code when using a simple feed pulled directly from Zazzle, so you will not have any reports to evaluate individual social media site performance. For example, you won't know if Facebook or Twitter brings your more sales. But this is not a big enough reason to avoid using IFTTT. The site can increase your potential for both Royalties and Referrals, the latter of which can help you reach a Volume Sales Bonus. Not to mention, that once it's set up, you won't need to spend much time here, because auto-posting generally takes care of itself.

When you begin to create auto-posting recipes on IFTTT, you will be prompted to connect each applicable social media network. Begin by clicking *Create*. Next click the word *This* (in the phrase If This then That). Choose the *RSS feed* icon. Your feed URL is the trigger. Click *New Feed Item* (triggers when a new item is added to your feed) and enter your customized RSS feed URL.

If you feel a little overwhelmed and don't want to go review the RSS feed pages, here's a simple URL that you might use to get you started:

http://feed.zazzle.com/**StoreName**/rss?at=**00000000000000000**&ps=1&qs=**cat**&st=**new**&tc=**Blog**

- Change *StoreName* to your store name.
- Change the *zeros* above to your own Associate ID.
- The number 1 means one item will post.
- Change *cat* to a word used as a tag, title, or category in your store — or remove &qs=cat to pull any new item.
- Change the word *new* to *popularity,* if you would prefer to pull popular items.
- Change *Blog* to a tracking code (TW for Twitter, etc.).

Note: We suggest you keep your tracking ID coded in the URL, just in case the software might update and begin accounting for it.

Click *Create Trigger.* Click *That.* Choose *Facebook Pages.* Choose *Create a Link Post* (to link to Zazzle). In the *Action* section, you can add some customization. For *Link URL,* change it to {{Entry-Content}}. For the message area, add this (but change *StoreName* to your store): {{EntryTitle}} New Item #StoreName {{EntryUrl}}.

These settings can be changed at anytime. The message box is huge! You could conceivably add a paragraph of text and send it over to Facebook. Click *Create Action* to finish.

Repeat this again, but choose your Twitter account. The message box for Twitter needs to be short. You may wish to only use {{EntryTitle}} {{EntryUrl}}.

IFTTT checks feeds every 15 minutes. After you create a new item, check both Facebook and Twitter to see how the item appeared. To make adjustments, edit the message part and/or change your RSS feed query to pull a different selection.

Hootsuite

One limitation of using IFTTT, is it doesn't connect to Google+ Pages or Profiles. Hootsuite, however, does connect to a Google+ Business Page. Hootsuite has a free basic plan that allows you to connect up to five social profiles. The free plan should suit your needs because you only need to add your Google+ Page.

If you use our link to sign up for the free plan and you ever decide to upgrade to a paid plan, we would receive a small affiliate commission, so, please consider using this link:

http://KidsandMoneyToday.com/hootsuite

As with IFTTT, your tracking code does not pass through the auto-posting process, so your Referral Reports will not be able to distinguish the traffic and sales that come from your Google+ promotions. But similar to IFTTT, once this is in place, it will work on auto-pilot and increases your potential for referrals and sales, so the initial set-up time is usually worth it. You should still include a unique tracking code in your RSS Feed — just in case the software is ever updated and the code begins to carry through.

Here's an example of how the post will look when posted over to a Google+ Page:

To set up a RSS feed, you will go to your left menu *Settings >
RSS/Atom*. A screen pops up that looks like this:

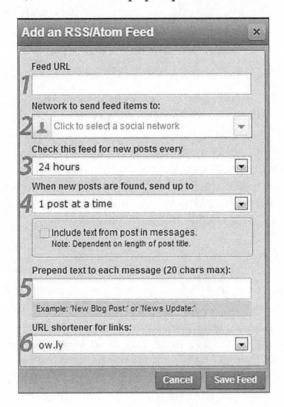

1. Enter your feed URL in the first box.

2. Select your Google+ page to send the feed to.

3. Hootsuite will check for a new feed item every 1, 2, 3, 6,
    12, or 24 hours. Choose every hour for testing. Keep in
    mind that Zazzle can take up to 24 hours to process Quick
    Create items so you may need to be very patient when
    waiting for your item to appear on your Google+ page.

4. Hootsuite can post anywhere from one post at a time
    up to five posts at a time. Start with one post at a time
    for testing. Later, depending on how active you are on
    Google+, you can decide if you can increase this with-
    out being spammy. You might also increase it to display
    matching items in a set.

Note: You can temporarily deactivate Hootsuite auto-posting. You might do that if you're using Quick Create and don't want to send items with the same image to Google+ all at once.

Include text from post in messages: If you check this box, the feed *will* pull in the price. If you do not want the price included, do not check this option. We like to leave the price off and hope the user will be curious enough to click through to see it.

5. You can *Prepend Text to each message* which allows you to add up to 20 characters of text to the beginning of each posting. This is a good place for a keyword with a hashtag or simply use something like "New Item." If you use your company name, it may help with branding. Try to keep your prepended text unique for each feed. This way you can track and troubleshoot any issues that might arise. Hootsuite automatically sends over the store name, pre-pended text, item title, and image.

6. You have a choice of URL shortener formats to use. All the choices are indicative of Hootsuite, so your viewers on Google+ will know that you are using auto-posting. This is another reason to lace your social media with some real human posts. While many Internet users are used to seeing some automation, visitors don't like to see a page where there is absolutely no human interaction. Who wants to follow a machine?

To correct or change an RSS Feed (image entry #1), you will have to entirely delete the RSS/Atom action and create a new one. However, at any time you can make adjustments to the prepended text, number of posts, and how often Hootsuite looks for new items.

One advantage of the Google+ social network is that you can edit your posts *at any time*. We recommend that every week or so, you go back into your Google+ business page and click *Edit* on all your automatic postings. Add a hashtag in front of a keyword. You might also enter additional keywords or synonyms with hash tags. This will connect your post to other Google+ posts with the same hash tag, and might refresh your post to bring in some new traffic.

Zazzle Automatic Promotion System (Zaps)

The first purchase we suggested was your domain name, even if you were not yet setting up a blog or website. The second purchase was business cards. Next you might purchase the Zazzle Automatic Promotion System (ZAPs) for a one-time fee.

When you use ZAPs, there is very little coding required. Most of it is fill in the blank, and you will also receive a slide show tutorial with video instructions to guide you along. Here's a consolidated list of what you can do using ZAPs:

1. *Pull Specific Products:*

    • From the entire marketplace, your store, or another store.

    • From a specific category, a specific gallery.

    • By query string - meaning by niche or keyword.

    • By popularity, price (ascending or descending), or date created.

2. *Choose a sort order:* Of ascending or descending (for pulls using "date created").

3. *Eliminate Terms:* Used to filter out spammy stores.

4. *Require Certain Terms:* Used for tightly targeted pulls.

5. *Include Store Owner Tags:* Beneficial for posting to blogs and for Search Engine Optimization (SEO).

6. *Retain Associate ID:* Keeps your referral when posting to:

    • Social media networks,

    • Email campaigns,

    • Blogs (Blogger and WordPress), or

    • Newsletters (tested with MailChimp).

7. *Customized tracking code:* Add your own to each feed.

8. *Choose your image size in pixels:* This image will pass through to Facebook, Twitter, Google+, and Tumblr.

9. *Choose a thumbnail size in pixels:* Used when posting to any site that uses thumbnails.

10. *Choose the background color:* Used behind the Zazzle design, this is beneficial for auto-posting to blogs where you want to match the background color on the page (branding).

11. *Ferris Wheel Rotation:* Rest assured that built in controls will reduce the chance of posting any duplicate items during a thirty day period (so your customer shouldn't see the same item twice).

12. *Control Post Times:*

   • Choose how often: Choose a particular day of the week, or post once every two days, three days, etc.

   • Choose how many posts per day: Once or twice.

   • Choose the time of day to post: Estimate down to a 15 minute time-frame of when your post will appear.

13. *Run in test mode:* View the output prior to going live.

14. *No Feed Limit:* Create as many RSS feeds as you like.

15. *Create posts with SEO Friendly Links:* All links use rel="nofollow".

16. *Venture beyond social media sites:* Auto-post to blogs and newsletters (such as MailChimp).

17. *Free Membership to a Google+ Closed Community:* Ask questions and share ideas with other members.

18. *Outstanding Support:* No question is too basic.

19. Bonus #1: A special feed to pull Zazzle coupon offers

20. Bonus #2: If you like affiliate marketing and want more, you have access to a customized Amazon.com product feed. (You would need to sign up as an Amazon affiliate.)

There is no software to install. ZAPs is designed to be used securely online to output a special RSS Feed based on user entries, but more importantly, it retains your tracking code. This means you will have valuable information to make better marketing decisions.

The second major benefit of ZAPs is it can auto-post to a blog. Zazzle store owners are currently using it with both Blogger and WordPress.

You can set it up to automatically create a live post or to create draft posts that you might customize with your own text. Usually, a blog full of Zazzle items will not be enough to rank well in search engines, so it's best to add additional text and surround your Zazzle posts with other posts of relevant content. But even if you did leave the site running on autopilot, you could occasionally share it out to your social networks. If you're not yet ranking in search engines, this should help bring you traffic.

ZAPs can also post to newsletters. You can add the advanced RSS feed to your MailChimp template and it can automatically add a relevant popular item to every newsletter you send out. If you opened your MailChimp account earlier and were wondering what to tell your subscribers. ZAPs will help you solve that problem. When Zazzle has a sale, you could easily change a keyword in your feed to pull the applicable product type and send out a coupon to all your subscribers.

As with all software, if any part of it has issues, whether it be the feed from Zazzle itself, ZAPs, or something on the social media platform that you plan to post to, then everyone along the path may have to adjust. You should expect that your designs will occasionally fail to post, but if you need any help troubleshooting, just visit the private ZAPs Google+ community.

For artists, ZAPs means you have more time to design or learn new software features like special effects and filters. Photographers have more time for photo shoots. For those focused only on the associate side of Zazzle—you'll have more time to research new audiences, trending topics, and more.

As always, your final income will depend on your personal designs and marketing efforts. ZAPs is a mechanism to produce a sophisticated RSS Feed, not a guarantee of sales.

ZAPs is a tool to assist you in completing the auto-posting process in an enhanced manner, saving you hours of time. It increases your opportunity to achieve a volume sales bonus and make educated marketing decisions.

If you use our link to sign up, we will receive a small affiliate commission, so, please consider checking the current price here:

http://KidsandMoneyToday.com/zaps/

PostPlanner

Once you have sales, you might also consider purchasing Post Planner. This is paid App that allows you to schedule posts on Facebook to your Profile and Pages, but not Groups.

The chart shows some of the features that Post Planner Offers:

Repeating Posts: The number one thing we love about Post Planner is you can schedule repeating posts. For example, you can schedule all your Valentine items to post on the fifteenth of January and repeat these post every 12 months until 2020 (or whatever year you choose). This is "Set it-and forget it" at its best!

We can also schedule a monthly post inviting viewers to opt-in to our newsletter. This may capture new people who have *Liked* our page. Since this posts repeats only once a month, our current viewers shouldn't mind.

We might also post favorite YouTube videos to repeat once a quarter with a message, "Did you already watch (VideoTitle)?" This varies our content and if it's our own video, it also adds new views (which is good for our social authority on YouTube).

We can do the same with important blog posts to refresh some engagement on our website pages. How about creating a blog post around Halloween containing spooky items and scheduling it to auto-post every September, for the next 4 years?

One Click: You can post with one click to several Facebook Pages and your Profile. If you found a great article that would appeal to your Zazzle Page(s) but also a Page you have on another niche topic, you can select multiple pages and with one click, schedule the post to each location.

The image shows five locations chosen, and you can see how the text will only have to be written one time. This saves a huge amount of time for people managing more than one page. You can also see the *repeat* option that we discussed earlier.

The *stagger posts* option allows you to shift the posting times so all the posts do not go live at 11:25 AM. When you check this box you can choose the number of minutes to stagger between the five page posts, such as stagger every 45 minutes.

View Schedule at a Glance: Facebook already allows you to view your scheduled posts (in your activity log) but you can't see all your Facebook page posts in one place. With a glance, we can see which pages need more attention.

The image easily shows that activity is missing on several days, and one Page has only one post scheduled in a eight day period.

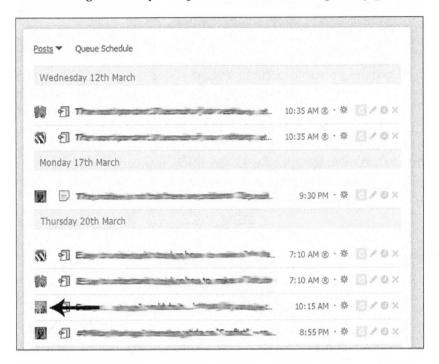

Link Posts: Post Planner is capable of creating a *Link Share Post*, a post with a nice big image and a link. Simply click *Publish as a photo* when creating your post.

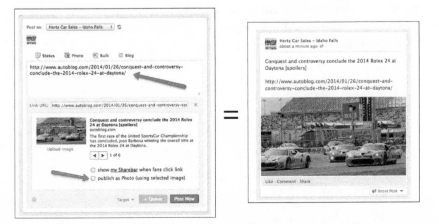

Curation Search Engine: Post Planner has a built in post curation feature. You can search by topic and find other items to share. You can sort by Trending, Blogs, Fan Pages, or Twitter.

When you find your niche areas, you can add them to your own personal "content engine" (which is like a filing cabinet). The articles in these files can then be further filtered by *most recent* or *most popular* articles along with an indication of their potential to go viral (based on the *shares* and *likes* shown in the lower right corner). We ran the sample screenshot below using the keywords of "trending travel" but you could easily run this for your own niche (weddings, new baby, etc.)

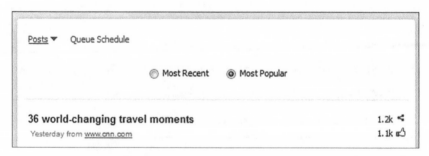

You have the option to create your own folder and add your own RSS feed from a blog, Facebook Page, or Twitter. You might add your store RSS feed. This means your content will be added to the search pool of information and others could potentially pull your content to share, especially if your feed posts have some indication that they are trending or popular.

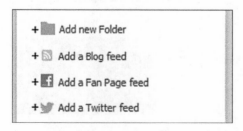

Status Ideas: A key element of being successful in social media is to mix and match the type of items you post to your page. This usually encourages viewers to engage, adds a human element, and simply makes your page more interesting.

Post Planner Status Updates help you do that. These updates will appear as text entries. Use them between your Zazzle posts to mix up the elements that appear on your page.

The *Status Ideas* area contains a database that you can swipe from and post to your page. You'll find a drop-down menu where you choose a main topic. Do you want to post a question, something that asks readers to fill in the blank, a deep inspirational thought, or something seasonal?

Choose your main topic, and the next screen proposes three suggestions for updates. If you don't like them, you can simply refresh to search for more. The software algorithm ensures you are not posting the same item recently chosen by another member.

When you don't know what to post, this area can solve your writer's block. In an under an hour, you can schedule status updates for the next month or even two or three months— depending on how fast you click and how often you schedule your posts.

Analytics: Simple analytics are included. Facebook has their own Insights (which you can use for free), but here again, we see that Post Planner pulls everything together in an advanced format.

You can review an individual page or all your Pages at once as a single screenshot—helpful when you manage multiple pages. You can choose the time frame: a week, 10 days, 2 weeks, 3 weeks, or a month, and then view your *Likes, Comments,* and *Clicks* as a percentage. This will easily let you know if people are even clicking through from Facebook over to Zazzle.

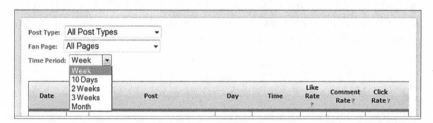

You can begin to evaluate the type of post that creates the most engagement. The first post below has a little image icon by the post title. As we might expect, an image post will have a higher click through rate (in this case 29.17%) than the other posts in the report. Days of the week and times are also displayed to assist you in further analysis.

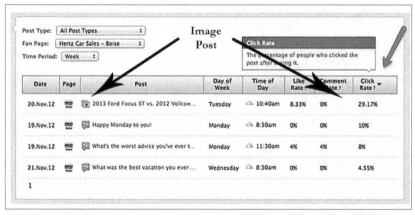

These are just the highlights of our favorite features. If you have any interest in this, please consider using our affiliate link:

http://KidsandMoneyToday.com/postplanner/

Buffer

Buffer is another auto-posting platform. Buffer can be used to schedule additional content for Facebook, Twitter, Google+, and other social networks. At the time of this writing, we've been unsuccessful using Buffer for sharing Zazzle items. In every case, one of the key elements would be missing whether it was a photo or the referral coding.

What Buffer is good for is mixing in a healthy number of related posts. We previously suggested that you aim for a ratio where the sum of all your articles, videos, and shared posts exceeds your number of sales pitch posts.

No one likes to be hit with ads all the time. When you have someone over for dinner, you usually show them the house or garden and maybe chat a little before sitting down to dinner. Social media is the same. You entertain your audience before showing them the main event. Buffer will help you entertain efficiently.

In most cases Buffer's free plan will suffice as it allows you to connect *one* Twitter, Facebook, Linked In, and Google+ page. You will have to choose either a Facebook Page or Profile, but if you're following our suggestions, you're already using just a Facebook Page to represent your business, so this should not be an issue.

Buffer has options similar to the other platforms. You can control the day of the week, time of day, and quantity of posts per day. You can pause all activity at any time. You can also run variations such as tweet 4 times a day on weekdays, but only 2 times a day on weekends. There is also a text box that allows you to prepend any post with your own thoughts. When possible, use your keywords and hashtags in this area. You can also choose your link shortener. If you choose bit.ly, people will know you are auto-posting, but not necessarily know that you are using Buffer.

Buffer has a browser App for Chrome and Firefox which makes it easy to schedule posts to social media while viewing the Internet. Once installed, often there is an additional *Post to Buffer* option that appears when you click *share* on websites. This allows you to take advantage of Buffer's powerful scheduling features. Now when you find ten items to share, instead of posting them all immediately, you can send them over to Buffer and que them to post over a period of time.

Buffer scheduling screenshot:

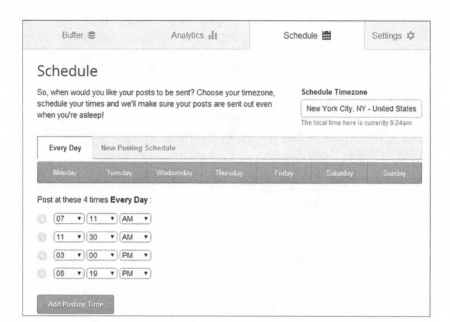

An additional benefit of Buffer is its simple analytics. You can see what type of posts perform well, and try to do more of those. Reports are customized for each social network. For Google+, it tracks clicks, comments, re-shares and +1s as shown below:

If you have no clicks, you probably need to take a second look at what assumptions you made about the interests of your target audience.

Each report is customized for features applicable to the social network. For example, if we pulled a Twitter Report, the analytics would show retweets, mentions, favorites, clicks, and potential reach (a combination of your followers and the retweeter's followers).

Buffer is free, so use it to add a variety of images, videos, and articles to your Facebook, Twitter, and Google+ Pages.

https://bufferapp.com/

Auto-posting Summary

As a quick summary, if you would like to use only free options, you can use IFTTT and Hootsuite with an RSS Feed to post automatically to the major social networks. We've confirmed that as of this writing your referral ID will pass through to Facebook, Twitter, and Google+, so implementing this process should increase your potential for a Volume Sales Bonus. You are essentially giving your business a potential pay raise because once set in place, the auto-posting should continually bring in income.

Use Buffer, also free, to schedule some variety between your Zazzle feed posts so the user sees more than a list of ads.

Once you have some income from Zazzle, we suggest you consider purchasing ZAPs for a one-time fee. ZAPs has the ability to create an enhanced RSS Feed that retains your Associate ID and tracking code when auto-posting. It's a powerful marketing tool that not only gives you access to tracking information to help you make better decisions, but can also be used to create blogs and newsletters that run on autopilot.

The Post Planner App is an enhanced Facebook post scheduler as well as a content curator with a monthly (or annual) fee. This gives you the ability to schedule repetitive posts and to post to multiple locations with one click. Their content curation system includes options to add your own feeds and select content from others based on targeted keyword, likes, and shares. This powerful tool saves you time searching the Internet for items to post and helps you easily create a unique mix of content for Facebook.

All these tools will help save you multiple hours of social media marketing. Efficiency is the name of the game. If you use our links to purchase access to either software, we will receive a small affiliate commission, so, please consider using our links:

ZAPs can be purchased at:
  http://KidsandMoneyToday.com/zaps/

Post Planner can be purchased at:
  http://KidsandMoneyToday.com/postplanner/

Tweaking Your Business

Community Participation

You should participate in the Zazzle community, in the forums. Try to check each forum daily, just as you would your email. A quick skim will be beneficial to your business because you will be alerted to any current issues. Also, try to Help others. When someone helps you, one way to show appreciation is to visit their store and clicking the *Like* button at bottom of their home page.

Many store owners report an increase in sales after visiting the forums. There are many theories as to why this might happen:

- Zazzle's algorithm has something in it that measures forum participation, such as activity or helpful posts.

- Every forum comment exposes your store to other store owners, who may take a look and this will increase your view count. Sometimes, they make purchases too.

- Zazzle associates find you in the forums and see that you are active, which is one factor playing a role in who they choose to promote.

- Every comment you make in the forum creates a link back to your store, thus playing a small role in ranking.

Browse the forums. Watch for store owners who post their best sellers, asking for additional promotions. This is an opportunity for you to create associate links to products that are proven winners (assuming the person posting is telling the truth). There is an entire forum entitled "Show Me" which is a great place to obtain new ideas. Also, associates might browse this forum, so consider posting some of your own designs in this area.

Occasionally you might try accessing the forum and receive a message to the effect of "You have tried to gain access to an area you are not allowed." This usually means you are not logged in, the thread you are trying to read has been deleted (or pulled from public viewing), or you clicked on a link to a forum you do not have access to yet (such as Pro-Sellers).

Increased Traffic: When you post in the forum, the link above your avatar will link to either your Profile or store. You choose this setting using the dropdown menu at the top of the forum:

When you set up a signature link, a little house image will appear at the bottom of every post you make in the forum:

Visit *My Account* > *My Profile* > *Member Profile* > *Social Networking:*

Account	Products	Images	My Account	Store	Associates	Earnings

Member Account

Account Settings
Order History
Address Book
Payment Methods
Comments
Zazzle Black Settings
Not for me
Member Profile
 Basic Information
 Interests
 Social Networking
 Stores
 Manage Profile

Member Profile: Social Networking

The addresses you enter below will be displayed as links in your profile.

Website URL:
http://

Facebook Page:
http://www.facebook.com/

The first box is a website URL, so you can enter your store here, but you might also list a blog you own if you are looking for traffic and links from Zazzle.

In this same area, you will also find entries for social networks. Go ahead and add those, if you haven't already.

Custom Banner

You can upload your own banner under *Account* > *Store* > *Content* > *Store Header Image.* This will appear on your home and category pages, but not individual product pages. The minimum size is 2360 × 400 pixels.

Consider adding your social media icons to your banner. They will not be clickable links, but might encourage visitors to look you up on the applicable networks.

Store Home Page Layout

Aside from adding a banner, you have the ability to add a *store* title, description, and tags. You can also customize the layout of your store home page. This is another area that you'll have to test and decide what works best for you.

You choose your design layout by going to: *Account > Store> Content > Edit Content.* Don't forget to click *Save* after making changes here.

Homepage Products
○ Show Products
◉ Show Featured Products
○ Show only the Categories Grid
○ Show only products from:

(Change | Clear)

> Featured Products

Categories
Categories must contain a cover image to be featured on the Store homepage.
☐ Show categories grid
▢ Show 4-up categories
▢ Show category titles in grid

Comments
☐ Show comment wall

You have four options for your home page: *Products, Featured Products, Show only the Categories Grid,* or *Show only products from* a specified category (which works well when promoting seasonal items). These settings can be changed at any time.

Many store owners choose *Show Featured Products.* To set a product as "featured," go to *My Account > Products* and click the *Action* drop-down option beneath the product you wish to feature. Choose *Add to Featured Products.* Featured items should receive a boost in views which may help improve your rankings.

Under *Categories,* you can choose whether or not to show your categories in the center of your store home page. If you want to rearrange your categories, go to *Products > All Categories,* and you will be able to drag and drop them to new locations.

When *Show categories grid* is left unchecked (as shown above), you will only show actual items on your store's home page. This keeps some products immediately visible to customers, above the fold — meaning the user does not have to scroll to see them. This may layout bring you more click throughs and more views.

How to Get a Large Image of Your Product

You might need a large product image without a watermark for a blog article or social media post. To capture a large image of your Zazzle product, follow these steps:

1. Sign in to your Zazzle account.

2. Open up the live public product page.

3. Click *Customize.*

4. On the left design menu, click the "X" to *View Large Image*

5. Right click and select *Save image as* to save your image.

This will give you a large image without a watermark. These steps will only work with your own products, which is a good thing. Zazzle is helping protect our images.

We'd suggest that you add text over this image before posting it live on the Internet (unless you don't mind it getting stolen). You could add your store URL, a motivational thought or how you would use the item—the main purpose being to mark your image in some way so it's protected.

Starting a Blog

Entire books have been published about blogging. Look for them and browse ideas online.

One key to successful blogging is to make sure you have content on your page. This means content besides the links to your Zazzle products. For Google and other search engines to rank your page, it needs to be *relevant*—preferably, more relevant than other pages on the Internet.

Your might write articles about topics related to the items you are promoting. Then, similar to what we've mentioned earlier, you would post these articles to social media in the hopes that they would be shared and bring traffic to your blog. This also creates links which helps rank your blog pages in Google search. Traffic to your blog would in turn lead to more clicks through to Zazzle and hopefully, more sales.

Every page in your blog should include links to all your social media networks. On Zazzle, you can add social icons to your banner, but these are not clickable links. These icons are more like *notifications* to look for you on these social sites. One advantage of blogs, is you can actually create links to click through and grow your social audience, which grows your social authority — which makes you more likeable by Google.

You should also add a Facebook Like box directly on your blog page. This will allow visitors to click *Like*, without even leaving your blog. Find the coding to do this here:

https://developers.facebook.com/docs/plugins/like-box-for-pages/

Check your other social sites to see if you want to use any of their sharing options. Google+ has a follow box. There are ways to add your Twitter feed to blogs and websites. Swipe the coding for these to quickly add some content to your blog.

If you are on YouTube, you can embed your promotional videos on your blog. Don't be afraid to put them on more than one page. Visitors don't visit every page, and if they see the same video twice, chances are they will just move on.

You can also embed other people's videos. This is another easy way to add content and encourage users to linger longer on your pages.

Look up how to set up Google+ authorship for your blog. This will give your articles a small boost in authority and may help you rank higher in search engines.

Engage with any visitors who leave comments. Be sure to thank them or provide them with your personal thoughts

Using your referral ID, add links to items from other store owners in the same niche. You could also swap articles with other bloggers. Look for a store owner with a similar blog (not a direct competitor but something related to your audience).

Lots of work? Absolutely. Blogging takes a lot of time, and you will have to decide if the Return on Investment is worth it. If you've set up some of the auto-posting options, you should have more time for quality blogging.

We suggested in the beginning of this book that you immediately obtain your domain name and have it redirect to your store. When you begin a blog, you will remove this redirect feature and choose a hosting platform, which may or may not be the same company that registered your domain. We will focus on using Wordpress to create a blog because it's fairly easy for beginners and has great potential for growth.

WordPress

Entire books are written on WordPress, so we will again focus on highlighting our best tips. We're fans of WordPress because it is so user friendly. It's a template where you can easily type an article and have it posted in minutes.

We suggest you *do not* establish your WordPress site using the free method on WordPress.com because it limits your potential for growth, ads, and basic control of your business. Simply put, there are things you can do with a WordPress.org site that you cannot do with a .com site.

You will need a hosting platform. We suggest you begin with BlueHost which is cheap and you can install WordPress with the click of a button. You don't have to know much about coding, which makes it very easy to get started. Their customer support is also very helpful in answering questions. Please consider using our affiliate link to sign up:

http://KidsandMoneyToday.com/bluehost

That being said, all hosting sites seem to have issues relating to some down time and slow loading pages. As our income grew, we eventually moved over to more expensive hosting and currently use WPEngine. They are a site solely focused on WordPress, with excellent support, security, and a good record of performance. We have an affiliate link for them as well. Find it here:

http://KidsandMoneyToday.com/wpengine

WordPress has something called Widgets and Plugins:

- *Widgets* are little blocks of code that you place in your side bars to either display information or accomplish a small task.

- *Plugins* are also made up of coding and usually accomplish more complicated tasks. They super charge your blog in some manner.

Add Rel="nofollow"

We previously discussed how rel="nofollow" should be included in all links that bring, or have the potential to bring, you income. Here are steps to add rel="nofollow" to the back-end coding of the Zazzle Store Builder Plugin.

You may need to ask a coding friend to assist you with this, especially if you are unfamiliar with transferring files to a server via FTP. If for whatever reason you are unable to complete these steps, the plugin will still work. Leaving it off might slightly impact your ability to rank, but other factors impact ranking too, so don't worry too much if you can't get this done immediately.

First, back up your blog. Next use a FTP program to locate and download the file called *zstore.php* from the *include folder*. Ours was located at: *Wp-content > plugins > zstore > zstore > include*.

Open your downloaded *zstore.php* file in your favorite editor and make a back-up copy.

We're going to add the nofollow coding by searching for the location of specific links. These will begin with <a href=" and we will insert the nofollow using this format: \"nofollow\". After making the change, the link will look like this:
<a rel=\"nofollow\" href=

• *Adjust the Title Link:*
Find this coding: if($showProductTitle == 'true') {

Directly below, insert the nofollow coding as shown here:
   $displaytitle = "<a **rel=\"nofollow\"** href=\"$link\"

• *Adjust Product Description:*
Find this coding: if($showProductDescription == 'true') {

Directly below, insert the nofollow coding as shown here:
  title=\"$description\"><a **rel=\"nofollow\"** href=\"$link\"

• *Adjust the ByLine:*
Find this coding: if ($showByLine == 'true') {

Directly below, insert the nofollow coding as shown here:
   $byline = "$by <a **rel=\"nofollow\"** href=\"$galleryUrl\"

• *Adjust the Product Price:*
Find this coding: if($showProductPrice == 'true') {

Directly below, insert the nofollow coding as shown here:
$displayprice = "<div class=\"productPrice\"><a rel=\"**nofollow**\"
href=\"$link\"

• *Adjust the Image Link:*
Find this coding:

<div class="gridCell" style="width: {$gridCellWidth}px; margin:0 {$gridCellSpacing}px {$gridCellSpacing}px 0;">

Directly below this, you will insert the nofollow, but *this time the coding is a little different.* The slashes are gone and it's like we taught you in earlier linking techniques. Add it as shown here:

<a rel="**nofollow**" href="$link" $analyticsLink class="realviewLink">

Save your file and using FTP, re-upload it to the back-end of your blog, back into the include folder. *Don't close the php file yet* because we will add tracking coding next. But first, check that your nofollow coding was done correctly.

Using your Firefox browser, open a live blog page with Zazzle products inside. Right click and select *View Page Source*. In the pop-up window, choose *Edit >Find* and search for *rel="nofollow*. You should see the code by your Zazzle links as highlighted here:

```
318  <!-- Products by Zazzle Powered by Premium Zstore Plugin. For more inf
319  <div class="allGrids clearfix">
320      <div class="centerGrids" style="width:490px">
321  <div class="clearMe"></div><div class="clearMe short"></div>
322                  <a rel="nofollow" href="http://www.zazzle.com/putu
323                  <div class="gridCellInfo">
324                      <a rel="nofollow" href="http://www.zazzle.com/
325
326                  by <a rel="nofollow" href="http://www.zazzle.c
327
328              </div>
329          </div>              <div class="gridCell" style="width
330              <a rel="nofollow" href="http://www.zazzle.com/putu
331          <div class="gridCellInfo">
332              <a rel="nofollow" href="http://www.zazzle.com/
◀ [.... m. ]

rel="nofollow          ∧ ∨

Line 318, Col 22
```

Adding Tracking Code

Tracking code is also not built into the ZStore plugin. To add the &tc=code into Zazzle Store Builder, we again need to change a link of code in your downloaded *zstore.php* file.

• *Adjust the Product Price:*
Find this coding:
> $link = str_replace("&ZCMP=gbase", "", $link);

Replace the line above with the following code:

$link = str_replace("&CMPN=zstore&zbar=1", "&C MPN=zstore&zbar=1&**tc=code**", $link);

Edit *code* to whatever you want to use to track the click, such as an abbreviation for your blog.

Save your file and using FTP, re-upload it to the back-end of your blog, back into the include folder.

Check your Associate ID and tracking code.

Inside your Firefox browser, open a live page containing Zazzle products and scroll your mouse over any Zazzle link. Look down to the bottom left corner, and you should see the long URL that this link points to. In the coding, you should see your Associate ID and tracking code as shown in the image below:

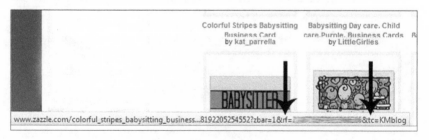

Scroll over all types of links that you use (title, image, byline, description, and price) to make sure you changed them all. With this change, you can track your referrals from your blog.

More Ideas

Inventory

Zazzle has a wholesale program. You should email support to obtain information if you become very serious about carrying and selling inventory.

If you only need occasional inventory for an event such as a local fair, you might simply take advantage of Zazzle's great sales combined with your associate referral commission. To do this, wait for a Zazzle sale and use the coupon along with your referral URL to make the purchase. If you purchase items at 75% off and resell them at normal retail price, you're making 75% profit, plus a 15% referral on the discounted price (not accounting for shipping costs).

Suppose you live near a historical site that has a gift shop. Assuming it was legal to photograph there, you could create custom products to meet a local demand. Little gift shops are perfect for this sort of thing. You might also carry inventory if you did freelance work.

One word of caution: you don't want to end up with a closet full of inventory. It is *always* better to run out of products than to have excess items sitting in a closet. Inventory is cash sitting on the shelves, cash that could be invested in growing your business. Start small with maybe five items and reorder when those sell.

Should you sell on eBay, Etsy, Amazon, or another third party site? Run the numbers. If you carrying inventory to sell on a third party sites, they will want a cut from the transaction. You will find an audience there, but again, we think you would need to take advantage of Zazzle's great coupons to be profitable.

When you run your calculations, be sure to factor in something for the time it will take you to list the item, hold the inventory, ship it in/out, handle any customer issues, and so on. Plus, if the buyer pays you through PayPal, this is another participant in the line of sale that will want a cut from your profits.

Will it be worth it? Maybe. But, it's certainly not passive income. You'll become part of the processing that completes a sale, and this is one thing, most people join Zazzle to avoid.

Advertising

We suggest you stay away from advertising until you've exhausted most of the other ways to promote your business. As we've discussed in this book, we think it's better to spend your profits investing in your growth, using social media tools or plugins. Our reasoning is that advertising can be a waste of hard earned dollars.

Money is wasted when business owners don't know: how to run an ad, who to show it to, how much they should consider paying for it, and how to track results.

If your business has grown and you feel you would like to try paid advertising, you might consider both Facebook Ads and Google Adwords. If you can afford to hire someone with proven experience, that would be even better. Both Facebook and Google Adwords allow you to fine tune your ad to be sent to a tightly targeted audience.

If you're doing this on your own, you would probably use Google's Keyword Planner to do research:

http://adwords.google.com/KeywordPlanner

This tool can help you find trending keyword phrases that have high monthly searches. You can also see how much competition the word or phrase has. You're attempting to narrow down your target audience so you can tell Google or Facebook to show your ad to people who will actually purchase from you. You can add additional filters such as age, demographics, male/female, etc.

Google Adwords also has retargeting features that you can take advantage of. This means you can target a visitor based on their past experience and actions. Maybe you want to advertise only to people who have visited your blog or your YouTube channel.

Facebook has something similar to retargeting. You can run an ad that would be shown to people who liked a certain page (and it doesn't have to be your page) or have particular interest.

When it comes to advertising, think outside the box. You might pay another site to display your ad in their newsletter.

Also, try the power of networking. If you've grown your list, you might join with another business owner and market to each other's lists. This free advertising—a promotional barter swap might work well for you.

Analytic Reports

Often, many people use analytics as a feel good/feel bad tool. In other words, they look at their stats and feel good, or they look and feel bad. This process repeats over and over again with no actions taken. We don't want this to be your story.

There's a reason analytics are toward the back of the book. You shouldn't spend too much time chasing analytics. However, tracking your results helps you make educated marketing decisions. You want to measure where you are currently at and to make changes based on predictions.

Also keep in mind, it takes about the same amount of time to promote any item, so assuming you can complete the sales conversion, your time is usually better spent promoting higher priced items, such as a handbag instead of a postcard.

Analytics is about predicting and testing, again and again. You might keep some sort of business journal. Try the old fashioned way: print a report with a date, write the action taken on it, and file it in a binder.

As you focus on different reports, always remember that your end goal is *conversions*. Don't get distracted trying to increase *Likes*, views, or comments when the conversion is more important.

Comparing Stores

It's not a very good idea to compare another store's performance with yours unless you are comparing stores of the same niche, who's owners work the same hours. How can a flower store compare its performance to a store containing political items, especially during an election year? How can we compare a store owner who works one hour a day with one who works full-time?

When we say, "Don't compare," this doesn't mean, "Don't look." As you view your own statistics and read success stories in the forum, you should continue to evaluate your target audience and see what else you might tweak to increase your sales.

Swipe and alter. If a wedding store reports selling 1,000 items, ask yourself what did they do that you might implement in your niche? Can you swipe the idea, but alter it to bring in more sales?

Views by Product

To see your Report:

- Go to *My Account* > *My Products*,

- Use the Sort drop-down menu to choose *Most Views* (by day, week, month, or all), and

- Look underneath each item for the *very light* grey font that shows your number of views

It has been said that this "views reporting" is not 100% accurate, but it's still an indication as to whether people are seeing your product. Views do not always equate to sales (because people do browse around); however, if your item doesn't get viewed, no one can buy it.

Views usually mean you are ranking well in the marketplace, but if you are also promoting the item on social media sites, some views could be a result of your own marketing efforts, your own shares to social media.

Views will not match your visits inside Google Analytics, because Google Analytics does not measure marketplace views. Google Analytics only measures your store URLs (your home page, categories, and departments).

You might divide your number of views by the number sold to give you a rough idea of how many times an item might need to be seen before it converts to a sale.

Take Action: Go to *All Products* and sort by *Most Views (month).* This will give you an idea of what is *trending* in your store, what has been popular during the last month.

Leave the default setting to show 24 items and print the results. (This will use several sheets of paper.) When you print it out, the format should change from grid to a list layout with blank space next to each item. This works well for making notes of the actions you will take. Look at the views for each item. Choose some items that you would like to increase the views on. These could be your favorites, but may also be high royalty items.

Analytics is about making a prediction based on a change. Choose something to change that you predict will increase your views. Make only one change so you can monitor whether it had any impact.

What should you change? Here's a short summary of some of our previous optimization and marketing ideas, plus a few more:

1. Optimize your title, tags, and description. Target long tail keyword phrases. Use plural and singular forms of a word, colors, or emotional words (like scary).

2. Set the item as a *Featured Item* in your store and drag it to a position "above the fold" (meaning the user will see it without scrolling).

3. Turn on *Show Latest Products Created* and *Show Latest Products Sold* (found under your *Store > Manage > About Page*)

4. Refresh your description: new words, links, or a flash panel.

5. Link to the item from another product description.

6. Post the item to several social media networks, especially Pinterest where people click and share a lot of images.

7. Ask people to share your item — literally ask them.

8. Consider changing the Zazzle *Category, Event/Occasion,* or *Recipient* to see if this might increase exposure.

9. Start a newsletter, an email campaign, that includes links to the item.

10. Advertise (begin with Adwords and Facebook Ads)

Write the date, and action you took next to each item. Recheck your views in a week. Evaluate and make a new prediction based on the next change you will make. Repeat the process.

Linkover History

Here's Zazzle's definition of linkovers:

> "Linkovers are a count of how many times a referral link you have created is clicked on. A referral link is an external link to a product, store, or other page on Zazzle that includes your Associate ID."

This report is found in the left margin of your *Associates tab* or at: http://Zazzle.com/my/associate/linkoverhistory

You can only see the number of click throughs. You don't get anymore information. Not where they clicked from, whether the click made a sale, nothing—so we don't spend much time here. Hopefully, it's a *feel good report* for you. Hopefully, you see some referral clicks coming through and hopefully, they are increasing.

Google Analytics

In the beginning of the book, we had you set up your Google Analytics tracking code at *Zazzle Account* > *Store* > *Settings* > *Edit Settings*. Google has been pulling statistics all along and now you can review them to make predictions and take actions to grow.

As mentioned earlier, Google Analytics records visits to your store pages. This means visits to *your home page, department, and category pages,* but not your individual product pages, because these URLs do not contain your store name or your Google Analytics tracking code. (Also, keep in mind that if you're sharing someone else's item with your referral code, these marketing efforts are also not tracked by your Google Analytics.)

Analytics often tell us what's trending, what was popular with our visitors and what keywords they used to find us.

You can also use trending topics to boost your sales. You might sign up to receive alerts for your targeted keywords, which could give you ideas of new products to create. It's free, and found at:
http://google.com/alerts

To introduce you to Google Analytics, we will look at some basic simple reports. Additionally, here's a link to the entire Google Analytics help directory to assist you further:
http://support.google.com/analytics/?hl=en#topic=3544906

What are your most popular landing pages?

Your landing pages that receive the most visits are your doorways, the place that your site is letting in or attracting the most traffic.

See your report:
• Go to *Google Analytics* > *Behavior* > *Site Content* > *Landing Pages*

Here's a screenshot of the menu items in this report:

Take Action: Look for pages you've promoted. Brainstorm actions you might take on pages that are missing, actions to increase visits to these pages that you want people to land on. Be careful how you interpret high bounce rates (visitors who enter and exit on the same page), low page views, and low duration. If these people clicked over to Zazzle to buy a product, this is a good thing.

Where did the visitor come from (what was their prior page)?

You can filter your landing page report for more information:
   • Add the *Secondary Dimension*: *Behavior* > *Full Referral* to show the full URL page prior to the landing page.
   • Add the *Secondary Dimension*: *Behavior* > *Exit Page* to show the page the visitor exited from, meaning the page they viewed last. (This is not the page exited to, not the page the visitor landed on after leaving your site.)

Take Action: What site sent people to your landing pages? Evaluate the pages doing well. Is there things you should do more of? Do you want users to go to a certain page? Send more links to those pages. Assuming your exit pages do not correlate to sales, you might add links to these pages enticing the visitor to click something else. You might also rearrange your exit pages, bury them deeper in your site making them harder to find since they lack interest, and then see what new pages people exit from.

What social networks are sending visitors to my website?

Earlier, we suggested you establish your social media networks and begin sharing your department, storefront, and category pages using both your referral and tracking code.

See your report:

• Go to *Google Analytics > Acquisition > Social > Overview*

If you show no social data, widen the date range or check that your analytics coding is set correctly. This report will show your storefront page, departments, and categories.

Here's an example of a report showing social network traffic.

Take Action: To increase traffic, try sharing your store, department, and category URLs more often. Take note of which social network brings you the most traffic. Next, click on a specific social network to see which URLs were shared. Which category or department brought in the most clicks? Have you sold any items in that category? Sometimes the social site sending the most traffic, does not necessarily send *buying* traffic.

Make a change that you predict will increase your social click throughs. Evaluate and repeat the process.

Which social media site sends engaging visitors?

View your *Network Referrals* report to see engagement metrics like: Visits, PageViews, Average Visit Duration, and Pages/Visit.

See your report:

• Go to *Google Analytics > Acquisition > Social > Network Referrals*

Here's an example of a report showing social network referrals.

Take Action: This report might help identify the type of audience you're attracting.

In the above report, the LinkedIn visitors spent more time than the Google+, Facebook, and Meetup visitors, but the Meetup visitors viewed the second highest number of pages, meaning they browsed around the most.

Explore the *Secondary Dimension* to add other factors. For example, segment by *Time > Day of the Week* and you might see what days pulled the most click throughs on each social site. If you have been posting twice a day for the last month and see that clicks only come on Thursdays, you might test what impact posting three times on Thursdays would have on your sales.

If you segment by *Acquisition > Referral Path*, you might see your Pinterest pins that generated a click through. This can help you decide what type of images to pin on Pinterest to bring you more traffic.

Make a change that you predict will increase one of the measured factors: visits (click throughs to your site), visitor duration (time on site), or number of pages visited. Evaluate an repeat the process.

What keywords did visitors use to reach your site?

See your report:

• Go to *Google Analytics > Acquisition > Keywords > Organic*

Here's a screenshot of the menu items in this report:

Take Action: Organic means these are words people used to find your store pages through Google search. Are the keywords you targeted on the list? If not, why might they not be performing? Are there keywords you didn't think of? Are they buying keywords? Should you add them to your titles, tags, and descriptions?

Which pages did visitors using those keywords land on?

See your report:

• Go to *Google Analytics > Acquisition > Keywords > Organic > Secondary Dimension > Behavior > Landing Page*

Here's a screenshot of the menu items in this report:

Take Action: You make your store pages *relevant* to search engines (organic search) by ensuring the content within is relevant to the search terms (words). Should you rearrange products? Create new categories? Adjust text? Try to get more inbound links?

Make a change that you predict will impact this report. Evaluate and repeat the process.

What's the path my visitor takes?

See your Visitor Flow and Behavior Flow reports:

- Go to *Google Analytics > Acquisition > Social > Visitors Flow*
- Go to *Google Analytics > Behavior > Behavior Flow*

These two reports will have the format shown in the image below. The *Visitor Flow Report* will begin with the social media network your visitor came through on. (The *Behavior Flow Report* will begin with the URL the visitor landed on.)

Visitor Flow Report showing traffic flow from social media sites.

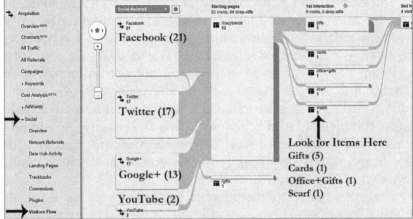

Take Action: Look deeper than the network that is bringing traffic. What category or department is popular? In the image, you can see the items of cards, scarf, and watch. Depending on the time frame pulled, this area might indicate a trend in your store.

Is there a path that surprises you? Are the customers going where you desire? A watch is a better sale than a note card. You might take actions to promote categories or departments containing more expensive items to bring you higher royalties.

The *Behavior Flow Report* (not shown) will show you specific URLs. Take a look at the drop-off pages (exit pages). Have you had sales in these areas? This might indicate they are dropping off onto a product, which is a good thing. If there's never been a sale, maybe these are pages that need improvement. The interest was there, but the customer didn't buy—why did you lose the sale?

Make a change that you predict will improve the traffic paths or customer experience. Evaluate and repeat the process.

Tax Advantages for U.S. Sellers

The following tips apply to U.S. citizens. We suggest everyone read through it and check if you have any similar rules that might boost your income in your own country.

U.S. Tax Laws

There are many tax advantages for U.S. citizens owning their own business.

You can protect your identity by obtaining an Employment Identification Number (EIN) to use instead of your Social Security Number (SSN). The Internal Revenue Service (IRS) assigns EINs to business entities. You enter it in the box that asks for your SSN.

When you file your tax return, you are not an employee of Zazzle, but an independent contractor. Zazzle will issue a Form 1099 reporting your sales to the IRS. Sole proprietors using Zazzle must complete a Form Schedule C. The IRS requires you to pay 15.30% self-employment tax (12.4% for social security and 2.9% for Medicare) so it is very important that you set aside this amount from your Zazzle profits.

The simple need-to-know fact is: whenever you can write off eligible business expenses, you lower your taxable income and pay less taxes. This equates to more money in your own pocket.

The first large tax deduction you should attempt to qualify for is the business use of your home. Is there a room you are not using that you can designate *exclusively* for business? Do you have an eat-in kitchen and a dining room that you never use? To qualify for this deduction, most people have to move some furniture around. The dining room chairs would have to go, but the table might become your new desk. Bookshelves could come in and curio cabinets would come out.

You might also make your guest bedroom your new office, but your office must be used only for business, so the bed must come out and visitors would have to sleep on the couch.

Suppose you have a 2,000 square foot home and your business area is 10% of the square footage of the entire home. If you pay $1,000 a month for the mortgage (or rent), then you can write off $100 (10% x $1,000) per month as a *home office* expense. This is

$1,200 a year and you haven't even accounted for other related home expenses like electricity and utilities.

The IRS expects a business to make a profit during 3 years out of a 5 year period. We suggest you try to *always* have a profit. After all, that's the main reason you are in business to begin with—to earn an income. If you are following our suggested Zero Balance Business Plan, you can figure out a goal for your annual income. Using our example, if you want to deduct a $1,200 home office expense, along with your annual domain name expense, business cards, ZAPs purchase, Post Planner, and your required portion of self-employment tax, this sum would be your annual goal.

$_____ (Estimated annual domain name purchase)
$_____ (Business cards purchase)
$_____ (ZAPs purchase)
$_____ (Post Planner purchase)
$_____ (Estimated self-employment tax set aside)
$1,200 (estimated home office expense)
Total business expenses (Your first goal for annual income)

If you are aiming for a zero balance, this is an easy way to come up with an annual income goal. This is just your minimum goal.

Of course, you want to earn more than your bottom line expenses. But, suppose you did only earn enough to zero balance. The business has just paid $1,200 of your living costs. You are perfectly justified in cutting two checks to pay your $1,000 mortgage, one for $900 from your personal account and one for $100 from your business account. You have shifted $100 of *personal* expense into a *deductible business* expense. This means, while the business is zero balancing, you have extra money in your personal account. Plus, either you don't pay taxes on your business income (because your business income is zero) or you've just reduced your business income (which means you pay less taxes). Either way, it's a win.

We know most people starting a business on Zazzle will not immediately earn enough to cover the *home office* deduction. So, you don't have to jump right in and create an office in your home.* You might wait until your Zazzle income starts to consistently roll in. Then, begin looking for ways to reduce your tax obligation and keep those funds in your own pocket.

It is possible to immediately write-off a home office and declare a loss on your taxes, but if you declare a loss during 3 out of a 5 year period, you increase your chance of an IRS audit.

Kids on Zazzle

Zazzle is great for kids who love art whether it's photography, drawing, painting, or digital design. Even kids who are creative writers might generate some sales by placing their witty phrases on T-shirts, cards, and more. Put a camera in the hands of a child and they might surprise you. We didn't think too much about my son photographing the trunks and locks in our home—until he told me he had several sales of his "Secret Recipe Binder."

http://www.zazzle.com/family_recipe_binder-127188924620420798

Zazzle can teach creativity, math, entrepreneur skills, and more, while developing independence and self-confidence in your child.

There are two main paths for kids to earn an income using the Zazzle platform:

- Your child can own a store in which he or she is an independent contractor for Zazzle (i.e., a self-employed child)
- Your child can work for you
  - As a volunteer, or
  - As a paid employee

Your Child Owns a Store

Owning a store on Zazzle is a wonderful opportunity for kids to earn income. Your child can follow all the steps outlined in this book, just as you did. When you register an account on Zazzle, the form asks whether you are age 13. In the Zazzle User Agreement under the section titled *Age and Geographic Restrictions*, you will see that account holders must be at least 13 years of age to use the site.

> "You must be at least 13 years of age to use this Site.
> Please contact us if you have any concerns or questions
> about this restriction."
> (http://zazzle.com/mk/policy/user_agreement)

If your child is age 13 or older, your child owns the account and for tax purposes, your child will report the income. For U.S. children, this *earned income* can be placed in a Roth Individual Retirement Account (IRA) and saved for the child's future. (The contribution limit for 2014 is $5,500.) You can learn more in *The Kid's ROTH IRA Handbook* found on Amazon.com.

The second huge advantage of kids saving in Roth IRAs is that money held in IRAs is an excluded asset when seeking to qualify for federal student aid. The rules and more tips for federal student aid can be found in *How You Can Maximize Student Aid*, also found on Amazon.com.

Using those two books, together with this one, parents can create a process by which the entire family has greater financial stability. Imagine if you had a young child and could save $5,500 a year that did not count as an asset for computing federal student aid?

If your child is under age 18, he or she will need to be paid by check from Zazzle. This is because PayPal's user agreement requires users to be 18 years of age:

> "Eligibility. To be eligible to use the PayPal Services,
> you must be at least 18 years old and a resident of
> the United States or one of the countries listed on the
> PayPal WorldWide page."

http://PayPal.com/us/webapps/mpp/ua/useragreement-full#1

PayPal does have an option for parents to open student accounts. You might look into that as well, but it's just something you would have to change again when your child reaches age 18. So unless there is a rush for payment, it may be easier to just wait for the child's check to come in the mail.

We also prefer not to mix parents and students together in a legally binding contract. It's too easy to forget that you have a joint account with your child. Plus, sometimes our children can surprise us, and we wouldn't want you to have any unnecessary financial liability.

Your Child Works for You

You can also make this process work for a child who is not yet age 13, by having your child work for you. Your child can be a volunteer in your business. Under this business model, you would never pay your child. He or she would just be helping mom or dad with the family business. This requires no paperwork at all. Your child would still learn and gain self-confidence. However, there is no *earned income,* which is required for IRA contributions, so you can't take advantage of the Roth IRA and federal student aid rules. If you don't mind some paperwork, there is a better way.

The solution is to have your child work for you. To create *earned income* for your child, you put your child on your payroll. You could even employ your six year old. If your child can click, they can use the computer. You might pay your child to take and edit photos. If your child can draw, you could scan their items and pay your child for the time spent creating the drawing. There are buyers who look for child-like drawings. Why not give them a real one?

There are two ways to employ your child. Your child could help you with your current store(s), or you can open a separate account where *you would be the owner,* but all products would be created from your child's designs.

We suggest the later method. You may recall that we already suggest you always open a *new account* for all *new stores.* By using a separate account, you will eventually be able to transfer the entire store over to your child (when your child turns age 13).

When you open this new account, you will use a new email. You have to remember that you always have the ultimate responsibility for the Zazzle account—it is in your name. You own it. We suggest that you don't release the password for the email address or access to your Zazzle account to your under-age child. Instead, you can sit with your child and demonstrate how Zazzle works.

Any income generated for accounts in your name, will be *your income*. Zazzle will issue the tax form in your name because you are the owner of the account.

When your child is on your payroll, you report 100% of the Zazzle income as yours, and your business issues a Form W-2 to your child. Your income is reduced and your child now has *earned income*. This accomplishes two things:

- You will pay less taxes because you have just reduced your taxable business income.

- Your child can now invest in the Roth IRA that we mentioned earlier (because you've created the required *earned income* for your child). Plus, your family as a whole is able to shield this saved income from federal student aid calculations. It does not count as a family asset.

More details on employing your child and beginning child IRAs are discussed in the books previously mentioned. They include step-by-step instructions which are too long to include here, and since this scenario does not apply to all Zazzle store owners, we decided a short summary would be best for this book.

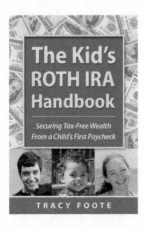

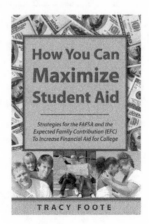

Zazzle is always coming up with new surprises.

Sometimes it's free business cards for Pro-sellers,
occasionally a $10 coupon, or
even a birthday card may show up in your emails!

Summary Checklist

Here's a checklist of suggested steps in priority order that we find has the potential to increase your income using Zazzle:

1. Research your Target Audience, a buying audience

2. Be realistic. Set reasonable goals while considering the competition and number of products already on Zazzle.

3. Choose your Business Name and register (purchase) your Domain name.

4. Open your first Zazzle account and store.

5. Establish Social Media Accounts such as:
   - Twitter
   - Facebook Page
   - Google+ Page
   - YouTube
   - Pinterest
   - LinkedIn

6. Open a list building account such as MailChimp and begin promoting your Opt-in URL to gain subscribers.

7. Prepare your store:
   - Create your Hidden Quick Create custom folder(s)
   - Create your Hidden Quick Create templates. Where possible, add your store URL as *Locked text* on these items.
   - Prepare images that you will use for designs.
   - Prepare a promotional image, something you might put on the back of cards or other items

8. Begin promoting other peoples products using your Zazzle Associate ID and tracking codes.

9. Set up the FREE methods of auto-posting to your social media sites.

10. Sign up for Google alerts for your keywords to monitor what's trending.

11. Begin Creating Products

    • Make some category folders to hold your *Public* items. Consider making a separate folder for each design, for easy bulk editing.

    • Allow your items to be customizable to increase your potential for income.

    • Begin making optimized *Public* products for the Zazzle marketplace. For optimization, consider:
        — Keywords used in your category, title, description, and Power Tags
        — Long tail keywords in the remaining tags
        — Keyword used in the name of your images
        — Steps to increase product views
        — Link building
            * Use *Events & Occasions* and *Recipient* options
            * Use HTML links in Zazzle descriptions
            * Share to social sites and blogs
            * Create a blog featuring items
            * Begin a newsletter or email campaigns
            * Create and promote Wishlists
            * Advertise on Facebook or Adwords

12. Create new templates as new products are announced.

    • Set them in a new Quick Create folder to bulk publish.

13. Print business cards and begin off-line promotion.

    • Attend local networking meetings:
        — Hand out your business cards.
        — Ask yourself how you might do what others are doing—but do it in your business model.
        — Collect business cards. Look these people up on social media networks and connect with them.
        — Send a thank you email and invite them to sign up for your newsletter.

14. Participate in the Zazzle forum community; help others and learn more.

15. Don't copy someone else's idea. You will have a better Return on Investment just promoting their product. You earn a 15% referral commission and don't have to spend any time creating.

16. Reinvest your income in the ZAPs program. Market items using your Associate ID and tracking codes.

17. Reinvest your income in Post Planner.

18. Research more ideas for marketing and product design. Browse:

    • Individual items in the marketplace
    • Forums, especially the *Show Me* forum
    • Other Zazzle stores
    • Blogs of other store owners
    • Social media sites of other store owners

19. Monitor your statistics: your analytics, views, marketplace position, traffic from social media networks, engagement on your social media sites, and do more of whatever appears to be pulling the best traffic and conversions.

20. Start a blog where you have full ownership and control, and if you use WordPress, use the ZStore plugin.

21. Consider carrying inventory and how much.

22. Consider using the API function (advanced coding, not discussed in this book).

23. U.S. citizens: Consider setting up a home office and taking advantage of other tax deductions.

24. Parents: Consider helping your kids get started on Zazzle to increase your family income, develop self-confidence, and educate. (U.S. citizens might take advantage of Roth IRA and federal student aid laws. More details are in *The Kid's ROTH IRA Handbook* and *How You Can Maximize Student Aid*, found on Amazon.com.)

25. Do something to promote on a daily basis, even if it's something small. Stay fresh. Create new items on a regular basis (a variety of designs and a variety of products). Just like a car, a store doesn't do well if it just sits with no activity.

Resources

The following resources (free and paid) may assist you with your Zazzle marketing strategies. For some of these links, we will receive a small affiliate commission, and we appreciate your choosing to use them. To view this list as clickable links please join our membership at:

http://KidsandMoneyToday.com/zazzle-member/

Google

- http://google.com/alerts
- Analytics Help
http://support.google.com/analytics/?hl=en#topic=3544906

Graphics

- http://canva.com/
- http://creativecommons.org/
- http://picmonkey.com/
- http://gimp.org/

Hosting

- http://KidsandMoneyToday.com/bluehost
- http://kidsandmoneytoday.com/wpengine

Keyword Tools

- http://adwords.google.com/KeywordPlanner
- http://ubersuggest.org/
- http://www.google.com/trends/

Landing Pages (templates for)

- http://KidsandMoneyToday.com/landing-pages/

List Building & Newsletter

- http://KidsandMoneyToday.com/mailchimp/

Mind Mapping Software

- http://xmind.net/

Social Media

- Buffer
  http://bufferapp.com/app
- Hootsuite
  http://KidsandMoneyToday.com/hootsuite
- IFTTT
  http://ifttt.com/
- Post Planner can be purchased at:
  http://KidsandMoneyToday.com/postplanner/
- ZAPs purchased at:
  http://KidsandMoneyToday.com/zaps/

URL Expanders

- http://expandURL.appspot.com/
- http://longURL.org/expand

URL Shorteners

- Bit.ly at http://bitly.com/
- Google at http://goo.gl/
- http://tinyURL.com/
- WordPress Plugin - URL Shortener with extras (paid):
  http://KidsandMoneyToday.com/track-link

Zazzle

- Help (search help) at:
  http://zazzle.custhelp.com/
- Associate Agreement
  http://zazzle.com/mk/policy/associates_agreement
- Associate ID (Find yours):
  http://zazzle.com/my/associate/associate
- Category Tree
  http://zazzle.com/assets/graphics/z2/pub/zazzle_category_tree_v2.01.zip

- Grouping
http://forum.zazzle.com/gallery/a_graphical_guide_to_grouping_aka_where_are_my

- Linkover History
http://Zazzle.com/my/associate/linkoverhistory

- Pro Seller Program Requirements
http://zazzle.com/sell/designers/prosellerprogram

- Products (direct links to create individual items)
http://forum.zazzle.com/tools/new_zazzle_design_tool_links

- Product Type List
http://zazzle.com/sell/affiliates/promotionaltools/rss

- Quick Create
http://zazzle.com/sell/designers/tutorials/qpctemplate

- Referrals
http://blog.zazzle.com/2014/03/24/make-money-with-referrals/

- Royalty Explained:
http://zazzle.com/sell/designers/nameyourroyalty

- RSS Guide
http://asset.zcache.com/assets/graphics/z2/mk/sell/RSSGuide1.03.pdf

- Tag Guidance
http://Zazzle.com/sell/designers/tutorials/tagging

- Tag Spam (Why Tag Spam Hurts)
http://forum.zazzle.com/create/why_tag_spam_hurts

- User Agreement
http://zazzle.com/mk/policy/user_agreement

- ZStore Builder Download & Premium Link
http://return-true.com/2009/03/zstore-helper-wordpress-plugin-for-zazzle-store-builder/

- ZStore Builder Guide
http://asset.zcache.com/assets/graphics/z2/mk/sell/tools/ZazzleStoreBuilderGuide.pdf

Index

Get Started on YouTube

Time saving tips to monetize your broadcast and create a repeatable video marketing system to generate evergreen traffic. Create video content based on business objectives and rank well to be found by your targeted audience.

A Video Channel is Easier than You Might Think...

Learn how to prepare and promote your videos so they rank for your targeted audience both on YouTube and in search engines. This book is chock full of information to help you get started fast. From channel set-up through basic analytics, this book is a reference guide of quick tips to help increase your sales conversions.

Major Topics include:

- *Prioritize:* Create videos based on analytical business objectives
- *Targeted Traffic:* Identify your customer and how they search
- *Rank:* Be found by your buying audience
- *Conversions:* Prepare video content to meet your monetization goals
- *Social Media Strategies:* Share videos properly to increase sales
- *Analytics:* Quick start to basic tracking methods including tips to get started with rank tracking, Google Analytics, and YouTube Analytics

Available for purchase at <u>Amazon.com</u>

Prepare Early to Qualify for Federal Student Aid

Save thousands of dollars by starting early with a plan for college. Find explanations for: all the components that determine federal student aid, the better places to save, and what you should think about come tax time.

Major Topics include:

— *FAFSA (Free Application for Federal Student Aid):* Detailed explanation of your *Expected Family Contribution (EFC)*

— *Tax-free and Tax-deferred Places to Save:* Explore investing options

— *Education Accounts:* Choose the right one and who should own it

— *Life Insurance:* Discover all the flexible uses

— *Single or Divorced Parent:* Valuable strategies for you

— *College Offers:* Distinguish between free money and debt

— *Tax Benefits for Education Expenses:* Make smart choices

Does your student have a Roth IRA yet?

Major Topics include:

— *Money Management:* Appreciate the benefits of a Roth IRA

— *Career Skills:* Identify different types of child employment

— *New Ideas:* Discover different ways parents can employ their children

— *Special Details:* Learn how parents can issue Forms W-2 for their child

— *Introduction to Taxes:* Basic tax concepts for children with low earned income

Become a Member of
Make Money Online Using Zazzle

You'll Receive:

- Zazzle news, videos, and online marketing strategies
- Access to links and other references that you might want to copy/paste from pages in this book

View the link below to join:
http://KidsandMoneyToday.com/zazzle-member/

Review Request

If you would recommend this book to others, please consider writing a 5 star review on Amazon.com.

How to write a review in four easy steps:

1. On the Internet visit http://amazon.com
2. Enter 0-9814737-6-8 in the search box on Amazon
3. About half way down, click *Write a Customer Review*
4. Please tell others what you liked about this book

Reader Comments and Inquiries

Comments, inquiries, or ideas for updates can be sent to us at
http://KidsandMoneyToday.com/Contact.
All remarks are considered for future editions and/or the website to further assist readers.

Find more online marketing tips and
links to connect with us on social networks at:
http://KidsandMoneyToday.com